Keep Moving
Forward

To Carol

Kimberly Wood Holland

Keep Moving Forward

Lessons from the Inca Trail

Kimberly Wood Dierwechter

Acknowledgements

For my three Inca warriors: Miguel, Saul, and Yossep, without whom I would never have survived the Inca Trail. There aren't enough words to thank you for all you have done. You gave me the courage and the ability to climb mountains. You are my heroes.

For Kellie: you are my sister, my protector, my friend, my listening ear, and my confidant who is always willing to listen to my fears and help me hold them. Thanks for believing in me when I said I could hike the Inca Trail.

For Kellie, Cindy, and Becky who shared this experience of a lifetime with me: I am so grateful for you all and I am so glad to have you in my life. I'm excited to see what adventures await for each of us, just on the other side of Machu Picchu.

For Russ: you see me so deeply, you help me know myself better. You give me confidence to do impossible things. I could not have written this without your encouragement and strength. Thank you.

And finally, many, many thanks to Tyler, Kellie, and Russ who took the time to read and edit this book and give me valuable feedback. This is a better book because of the three of you and I am grateful beyond words.

Introduction

"People don't take trips; trips take people." -
John Steinbeck

A few years ago, I wrote a book called *Everything I Need to Know in Life, I Learned from Singing Karaoke.* Charming title, obviously a riff on the popular book written a few years ago by Robert Fulghum. It's almost funny now how the book says EVERYTHING I need to know, but in retrospect, I feel like I knew so little at that point. When I wrote that book, I thought the greatest trial I could imagine was taking on a daunting new job. The book talks about the life lessons I learned through singing karaoke and how I applied them to taking on the job. And sure, it was a difficult job. But…c'mon!

I do still stand behind the principles of that book. And I still believe it was a crazy undertaking, to accept that new job. I wasn't just replacing someone who was retiring. I was stepping into the shoes of a giant, and I had to make my way with dwarf feet. The odds were stacked against me, for sure. But in the time since I wrote that book, my life has been ripped apart more times and in more ways than I want to count. I went through a divorce which was, admittedly, one of the most amicable and peaceful divorces ever experienced. Still, a divorce is a divorce. It's a dismantling of a life, it's the death of a dream, and it ripped me down to my core. I couldn't dwell on the ripped-apart feeling though, because I had two little people who were depending on me to usher them through this huge life change and to provide them with safety and security. I had no choice but to keep moving forward and keep figuring out my new life. In the process of that divorce, I bought a house all on my own. It was an exciting process to buy something like that all on my own, but it was terrifying. If something went wrong—if I chose a bad house, if the roof leaked or the furnace broke, or the foundation cracked into a million pieces—there was no one else for me to lean on. I had to solve those problems myself. I had to have a warm, safe, comfortable place for my children and me to live. Karaoke was supposed to teach me everything I needed to know in life, and yet…nothing in karaoke prepared me for those experiences.

Then, a couple years after my divorce, there came a weight almost too difficult to bear. I had fallen in love with a wonderful man named Ron, and I was planning my future with him. Not just planning: he was my future. He was my best friend and he was my emotional support as I navigated my new world. Then, one sunny Friday afternoon when we were on vacation at the beach, Ron drowned. In an instant, he was gone. We had been sitting there talking about our evening plans and our dinner reservations, and ten minutes later my world had ended. Instead of driving to dinner, I got to ride in an ambulance to the hospital while EMTs looked at me with pity in their eyes and continuously, tirelessly, performed CPR on the man I loved. Instead of being led to the table at the restaurant for our dinner plans, I was ushered to the small windowless room where three hospital clergy held my hand as an ER doctor told me they had done everything to save him, but they were unsuccessful.

Suddenly, I didn't have any more answers. If karaoke was supposed to teach me everything there was to know in life…why didn't I know what to do here?

Nearly three years after that day at the beach, I found myself at Kilometer 82, at the start of the Inca Trail in Perú. I was hoping to survive, hoping to make it to the end at Machu Picchu, and beyond that, I was hoping to find some sort of eternal spiritual enlightenment. I'm not sure I quite met that lofty goal, but I did learn quite a few lessons about myself through the experience. I feel like the Inca Trail broke me. Piece by piece, hour by hour of exhaustion, I was broken down. And now in the ensuing days and weeks as I process the experience, I am being remade new, filled with the enduring lessons of the trail. This book is a reflection on those lessons. I no longer believe I have all the answers. Karaoke didn't teach me everything, and neither did the Inca Trail. But make no mistake: the Inca Trail spoke to me. The Andes Mountains spoke wisdom to me. My hope is that all who read these lessons will benefit from my time on the trail and, in so doing, can be touched and changed by the sacred Inca Trail in their own way.

Chapter 1: What is the Inca Trail, anyway?

It will be midnight.
You will stand at a forked path,
flipping a coin in the air,
trying to decide which way to follow.
Your palms will weep moisture.
Cold winds will skitter down your back.

But these are the important things:
your foot poised above the earth,
your willingness to give it motion.

Over rough terrain you will travel
on the thin blade-bones
of your delicate tensioned ankles.

Carole Borges, "The Devil Speaks"

Most people have heard of the ancient citadel of Machu Picchu, perched high in the Andes Mountains. A few years back it was voted on the internet as one of the New Seven Wonders of the World. It's been on my bucket list to get there for years; probably since the first time I heard of it in middle school Spanish class.

A few years ago, my sister Kellie turned 40 and we decided to celebrate by going to a posh all-inclusive resort in Mexico. We spent our days running in the gym, taking salsa or merengue lessons, and then lounging at the pool (and pool bar). At some point during that trip, Kellie asked me where we were going to go for my 40th birthday. Seemingly without thinking, I said, "we're going to Machu Picchu!" And that was that. Once I say I'm going to do something, it's as good as done. I am just that kind of person. I said we were going to go, therefore we were GOING to go. Period. When I initially decided upon Machu Picchu, I don't know that I was thinking about hiking there. I'm not sure I even knew about the Inca Trail. Somewhere along the line in my hours of reading and researching, I stumbled upon the four-day classic Inca Trail trek and read that it was the best way to see Machu Picchu: to walk into the city at the end of a long hike. I thought, "This is it. That's what we are going to do."

To this day, I don't know what possessed me to think hiking for four days was a good idea. I'm not a particularly outdoorsy person. I don't camp. Before this trek, I hadn't slept in a tent since I was a teenager. I run and walk a lot for exercise, but I don't particularly do a ton of hiking, and certainly not for multiple days in a row. As if that's not bad enough, I tend to have a touchy stomach, so putting myself at the mercy of a tour company in a foreign country and whatever food they want to feed me was terrifying.

The summer before this trek, my then-10-year-old daughter and I went to the Dominican Republic on a mission trip designed for fifth and sixth grade children. We put on a series of Vacation Bible School programs at three different churches. The conditions were arduous. It was exceedingly hot, the bathroom facilities were very primitive, and despite being very careful about not drinking the water and using hand sanitizer, a virulent norovirus swept through our group, felling many to the twin tortures of vomiting and diarrhea. When I saw a fellow mom-friend from that trip about four months before my trip to Perú and told her about my plans to hike the Inca Trail, she laughed in my face. And not just a little laugh. No, she doubled over and couldn't stop laughing at the thought of me enduring that experience. When she finally got herself under control long enough to talk, she said, "Oh, you're going to die!" This woman knew me well. She was my roommate on the Dominican Republic trip and she knew how much I worried about catching the bug that was going through our group. And on that trip, we were staying in a hotel with an air conditioner in our bedroom. How much more of an anxiety attack would I have on the Inca Trail, sleeping in tents and enduring whatever the trail had to offer me?

So, it's not an understatement to say that this adventure was out of character for me. And yet, I was determined. I suppose I wanted to prove to myself that I could still do really hard things, even as I am turning 40. Maybe I thought it could be fun…? Mostly from all the articles I read, it seemed the hike was the only "real" way to get to Machu Picchu. Yes, we could take the train to the town at the base of Machu Picchu and then take a bus up to the citadel itself, but that seemed like cheating, so the Inca Trail it was.

Back to the original question: What exactly is the Inca Trail? Well, the Inca Civilization dates back to the 15th Century. I am no Inca historian and this isn't a history book, but I will provide some brief details. Under the leadership of the Emperor Pachacuti, sometime in the mid-1400s, the Inca empire grew from a relatively small organization to a massive empire encompassing parts of modern day Perú, Chile, Ecuador, and Bolivia. It was an impressive culture, to say the least. Their architecture and engineering was amazing to see, and to think that the buildings and ruins along the trail were created and designed some 500-600 years ago…it's mind-boggling. At some point during Pachacuti's reign, the citadel of Machu Picchu was constructed. They believe it was built as a summer home for the emperor, as the capital city of Cusco was higher in elevation and rather cold. Machu Picchu was still tucked up in the Andean cloud forest, but at a lower and warmer elevation. The Inca Trail was built as the road leading from Cusco to Machu Picchu.

The trail was considered sacred, as only Inca kings and royalty walked along it. The kings were carried in giant litters, held aloft by other Incas. Yale University professor and explorer Hiram Bingham discovered Machu Picchu in 1911. In his next expedition in 1913, as the overgrown jungle was cleared from Machu Picchu, the Inca Trail was discovered. There are a few different options for hikers now to hike the Inca Trail, but the classic four-day trek that we chose starts at the infamous kilometer 82 of the Urubamba River. It starts at an elevation of approximately 8,200 feet. For comparison, Denver Colorado, the highest major city in the United States, has an elevation of 5,280 feet. The Inca Trail starts some 3,000 feet above Colorado and goes up from there. The highest point on the trail (named Dead Woman's Pass, which made for lots of fun jokes) has an elevation of 13,828 feet. Clearly, this trail is no joke.

The Peruvian government regulates access to the trail. A maximum of 500 people are allowed to enter the trail daily: 200 trekkers and 300 guides, porters, and chefs.[1]　Hikers are not allowed to enter the trail independently; one can only hike this trail with an approved guide. This certainly wasn't a problem for me. I knew if I was going to be hiking this trail, I was going to need as much help as possible. We booked the trip in April 2017, a full 13 months early. Everything we read said that the Inca Trail passes booked up early since there was such a small limit for each day. Once we decided on the tour company and the time of year to go, there wasn't any reason to hold off. The decision was made. The research was complete. It was time to put our money where our mouth was, so to speak.

---

[1] Wikipedia contributors. (2018, August 11). Inca Trail to Machu Picchu. In *Wikipedia, The Free Encyclopedia*. Retrieved 02:33, October 10, 2018, from https://en.wikipedia.org/w/index.php?title=Inca_Trail_to_Machu_Picchu&oldid=854475723

Chapter 2: Preparation is Essential

"It's not the mountain we conquer, but ourselves." –Sir Edmund Hillary

I'm a planner. If you've read my first book, I cover that there as well. I like planning. I don't think that's crazy, I don't think it's absurd, I just am not the kind of person who likes to fly by the seat of my pants. Sometimes a little light spontaneity is nice (like maybe when I wait until I'm in the shower in the morning before deciding what I want to wear that day). But for important things, I'm just going to have a plan. Perhaps this is a manifestation of my anxiety somehow. If I plan and order my world, I don't have to feel as anxious because I have an idea of what my world is going to look like. Who knows, who cares; the fact is, I like a plan.

So when the decision was made to go to Machu Picchu, by way of the Inca Trail, it was time for some massive planning. I was about to undertake the single-most scariest thing I would ever do in my life. Merely thinking about hiking for four days straight and camping (in a tent!!) had my anxiety in overdrive, so my instinct was to make a plan for the plan and to plan out the planning process. I couldn't prepare enough. I started reading everything I could get my hands on about hiking the Inca Trail. We were planning to go sometime in 2018, but I started thinking and reading and planning all the way back in 2016. There were a myriad of tour companies who lead groups on the trail, there was a discussion about the pros and cons of hiring a personal porter to carry our things…so many questions, so many options. At the same time, our traveling group was expanding. Kellie was talking about the trip with her group of girl friends and Becky, her life-long friend, jumped in and said she wanted to join us. Becky had not travelled internationally like that before, so to say that this trip was outside her comfort zone would be a supreme understatement. But she felt something stirring within her, a sense that she needed to experience this hike, so she joined in. At the same time, I mentioned something about the trip to my friend Cindy and she immediately perked up. Going to Machu Picchu had been a bucket list item for her for years, and she was very interested in joining us. So, just like that, our group had doubled in size. More planning fun!

Kellie is much much more adventurous than me. She took a trip to China with her family and stayed in airbnbs, for crying out loud. But since this was my birthday trip and all, I put my foot down. If I had any hope of keeping my anxiety at bay, I was going to need an organized tour company to make sure that I was going to get out of this alive. I found a travel agent. I don't remember how; I just googled travel agents, and I think she was the first name that came up. But she was a gift, an absolute Godsend. She was so patient at answering all of our questions (and with four of us, we had a LOT of questions. Remember: I'm a planner. I think of all the questions.)

The decision was made, together with the travel agent, to select G Adventures as our tour company. They would provide everything we needed: guides, tents, personal porters to carry our belongings, chefs to cook our meals...it sounded perfect. All we needed to do was walk. How hard could it be? We also read up on the best time of the year to hike. The rainy season is from about October to April; that didn't sound fun. June-August was the busiest season, which we wanted to avoid. May sounded perfect. In early 2017, our four-person travel group was established, we had our travel agent, tour company and our timeframe picked out. There was really no reason to keep waiting, so in April 2017, a full 13 months before we were to actually leave, we pulled the trigger, so to speak, and booked the trip. Thirteen months later, we would meet up with our fellow travelers in our tour group, and it became a bit of a joke how early we had booked the trip. Yes, ok, it's true, 13 months is *possibly* a little bit excessive. But that's just how planners do.

So, this book is about the lessons the Inca Trail taught me, and I'm saying the first lesson is that preparation is essential. But I'm sure you're all wondering how it is that the Inca Trail taught me that when I've just gone on and on about what a planner I was already. First of all, I believe there is a bit of a difference between planning and preparing. Yes, we planned this trip early, we read everything, and ended up booking it very early—much earlier than our fellow travelers. But once the trip was planned, I didn't just sit back and wait out the 13 months. I put that time to good use and did everything possible to train and prepare myself for the hike of my life. Could I have done more? Sure. We can always do more in life, right? But I did quite a bit to condition my body. In the year prior to going to Perú, I trained and ran/walked two half-marathons. My thought was that if I could move my body for three hours straight for a half-marathon, I could probably hike for hours too. Starting about five months before the trip, Kellie, Becky and I began a fitness program that included cardio and strength-training exercises six days a week. We worked upper and lower body and did some pretty crazy high-intense cardio. (I still hate burpees.) I was still not in Olympic marathon running shape, but I had gone through hours and hours of workouts to train and condition my body. And on the trail, I learned a million times over how important that was. Never once did I think, "Man, I really over-estimated this trail. It's no big deal, and I WAY over-prepared." Nope. Quite the opposite, I thought, "WHY IS THIS SO HARD?!? I've been working out and preparing forever!!" But the point is, the Inca Trail taught me (perhaps not the first time I've learned this lesson) that yes, hard things are entirely possible in life, but we have to prepare. We can't just up and run a marathon tomorrow if we've never run a quarter-mile before. We can do it, eventually, but preparing is essential.

The thing about the Inca Trail that is different than just regular hiking and exercise is the elevation. It's no joke. This is another area where we learned just how important preparation is. Once again, we read up on everything. The G Adventures tour had two days planned into the schedule to acclimate in the city of Cusco, Perú. Cusco is at approximately 11,000 feet in elevation, which is high enough to affect most people. We read that two days isn't really adequate so our first act of preparation was to plan an extra day into the schedule. From what we read, the best way to acclimate was to take it easy, relax and let the body naturally get used to breathing the thin air without taxing it too much. Having that extra day in the schedule made this possible. In fact, we arrived early in the morning after three flights and trying to sleep on planes or in airports all night. So relaxing that first day was wonderful and essential! As soon as we checked into our hotel we immediately napped for a few glorious hours. It was lovely.

Secondly, we did our homework and three of the four of us got a prescription for Diamox before we left home. This prescription medication is supposed to somehow help prevent altitude sickness. My family doctor was skeptical that I really needed it, and typically I am not one to take medicine that isn't absolutely necessary. But in this case, I pushed for it. I knew if I was going to survive this hike, I needed to give myself every possible advantage. I couldn't go into it assuming that the altitude would be okay. Finally, our last act to prevent altitude sickness was to actively prehydrate our bodies before landing in Perú. We read that besides taking it easy for a couple days, the best defense against altitude sickness was to maintain hydration, which needed to start several days prior to even getting on the plane. I drink quite a bit of water typically, but I definitely stepped up my water drinking in the days leading up to the trip and then while there. More water? No problem!

Spoiler alert: all of our altitude preparation paid off. Perhaps it was the fact that we moved a little slower than some of the other members of our hiking group (and thereby gained altitude at a slower rate) but the four of us did not suffer from any altitude sickness. All around us, team members were falling ill left and right. The second day, one young Norwegian girl in our group was so ill, she couldn't stop vomiting. By that night, a handful of others had succumbed, and by day three, half of the team was sick. It's possible there was a stomach bug of some sort that was being passed around, so I don't know how many of the team were sick from the altitude. But we compared notes at camp each evening, and we discussed what altitude sickness preparations we had each taken. Many on the team had not given it much thought at all, and the fact of the matter is that the four of us who took altitude preparation extremely seriously managed to escape altitude sickness, thanks be to God.

So. While I've always been a planner, the Inca Trail reinforced the lesson about the importance of preparation. We can do all things we put our minds to, even the very hard things, but not without preparation. Once again, the Inca Trail is no joke. But it is possible to come out victorious, if one is prepared. So in life, whatever mountain is before us—be it literal or figurative—we must know that we can overcome it, so long as we prepare ourselves first. Preparation is essential.

Chapter 3: Over-preparation Can Be Dangerous

> *"We live in a wonderful world that is full of beauty, charm, and adventure. There is no end to the adventures we can have if we only seek them with our eyes open." -Jawaharlal Nehru*

So we booked our trip 13 months out. Our plans were set, and that left 13 long months to prepare. Fitness preparation was essential, and it was really good that I had that much time to get myself in shape as much as possible. But 13 months also gave us a LOOOOOOOOOONG time to think about the hike and worry about it. I read every blog I could get my hands on. I googled everything. I really do mean EVERYTHING. I don't think there is a blog article out there about the trail that I didn't read. Here is a sample of just some of my Google searches:

- Inca Trail packing lists
- Inca Trail elevation
- How fit do I have to be to hike the Inca Trail
- Inca Trail fitness preparation
- Inca Trail altitude sickness
- Overweight people hiking the Inca Trail
- Inca Trail failures

Yeah…I'm not super proud of all of those searches. It's one thing to read a blog article or two from someone who has hiked the trail, to get a first hand perspective about the experience. It's entirely different to actively seek out stories of people who tried to hike the trail and failed after the first day. I read those because I wanted to see something in them that would show me that I'm more fit or more prepared. But I didn't. The one article I read that stuck with me was written by a relatively active, fit couple. Looking at the pictures of them and then looking at myself in the mirror…I was not filled with confidence that I was any better. They talked about how they prepared by doing day-long hikes up mountains. I wasn't doing any of that.

Those stories started getting in my head.

Meanwhile, I spent months, together with my travel-mates, going over the list of things to pack for the trail. I don't hike and camp regularly, so I needed to buy EVERYTHING. I didn't have hiking pants, or boots, or long johns, or a daypack backpack, or a sun hat, or anything on the list, really. So that was a million things to obsess over; a million purchases to research and read about and plan and think. I read everything I could and then went straight to Amazon and bought everything. Everything the blog writer experts said I needed, I bought it. I even bought things I was pretty sure I wouldn't need, like water filtration tablets. We were told that the porters would boil and purify the water for us and I trusted that…but I couldn't help myself. I bought some just to be extra-extra safe. I was worried my knee would swell up (as it sometimes does when running) so I bought some portable ice packs. I was set.

When we packed for the trip, we packed all of our hiking supplies in our suitcase, along with regular stuff for the first few days in Cusco. A couple days before the hike, we had a meeting with the G Adventures tour company and we were given our duffel bags which the porters would carry. We were told we could pack 6 kg total for the porters to carry. Oh, and that included the sleeping bag we were renting, which weighed 2.5 kg. That left me a measly 3.5 kg (7.7 lbs) to cover all of the things I wanted to bring with me—all of the things I had spent 13 months amassing, after countless hours of research. Of course, on one hand, I didn't want to give the porters anything heavier to carry because they had to travel on the same trail, with HUGE backpacks full of my stuff. That hardly seemed fair or right. I wanted to be kind and compassionate to the porters. At the same time…7.7 lbs is not a lot of stuff. And the alternative was to put things that didn't fit into my own daypack that I would be carrying. I knew that my survival on this trail depended on me setting myself up for success, which meant carrying as light a bag as possible. So…this was a conundrum.

We got back to the hotel with our duffel bags and we were told there was a scale at the hotel that we could use to weigh our bags. So began a painful process. I went upstairs to my room and I started with the "best case scenario" of packing all of the things I wanted to bring in the duffel bag. All of the things I had read about for 13 months on all of the bloggers' packing lists. I wasn't being vain and trying to overpack a bunch of things I didn't need. Actually in my first go-round of items in the duffel I forgot to pack any shirts, so I definitely wasn't trying to overdo it on luxury items. I took it downstairs and weighed it with my fingers crossed. Surely this would be pretty close, right? I mean, it was the packing list stuff, plus a few essentials. I was dismayed to see that I was about 2.5 kg over. I had to seriously lighten the duffel bag. And then I remembered I might want to wear a shirt or two on the trail, so I really had to readjust.

The evening became a painful process of trial and error. Back up to the room, remove items, reconsider, rethink. Back downstairs, weigh the bag. Get sadder and sadder as I watch items I had carefully planned and prepared and purchased, being tossed aside. The water filtration tablets had to go. I begrudgingly chose to fully trust the universe and G Adventures and our guides and porters to provide healthy, safe drinking water. Similarly, the portable ice packs had to go—they were just too heavy. I decided to re-wear pants and t-shirts for multiple days and gave up my extra water bottle. Finally, at the end of a long evening of packing, I got the duffel bag to 3.5 kg. But I felt absolutely defeated and sick about it. I had planned so hard, I had prepared all of these things to bring, and I had spent 13 months dwelling on them. In an instant, they were gone. It made me extremely nervous for what was in store for me on these four days.

Maybe, just maybe, I had over-prepared a bit on the packing stuff. It's possible that with 13 months on my hands to prepare, perhaps I had a bit too much time and I went overboard. With less time to obsess about what should be in my duffel bag, maybe it wouldn't have left me feeling so defeated before we even started hiking.

But ready or not, feeling like I had enough "stuff" or not, it was time to start the trek. Miguel, our head guide, was supremely smart. So were his assistant guides, Saul and Yossep. But Miguel was brilliant. Not just about the trail—the Inca history, the flora and fauna along the way, basically any question we could ask him, he knew the answer. But more than that, I believe he was very astute about the psychology of Inca Trail hikers. He knew exactly how to handle our fears—even if we disagreed with his tactics, we came to realize how absolutely correct he was. Miguel had a system of telling us exactly what we needed to know, when we needed to know it, and not a bit more than that. You can imagine how well this sat with me, as a person who is kind of obsessed with planning and preparing. I wanted ALL OF THE INFORMATION! And I wanted it IMMEDIATELY! But Miguel stayed strong, and continued telling me what I needed to know for each moment, and nothing more.

The afternoon before we started the real hike, Miguel took the group on a "practice hike" in the town of Ollantaytambo. We were initially told that it was "optional" but at some point during the day, he made it very clear to us that we needed to be on that hike. So we were. If Miguel told me to be somewhere, there was no arguing with him. I was there. The practice hike was steep and a little scary, and he moved fast. I naturally ended up in the back of the pack and struggled to keep up and keep my breathing in check. This was our first time hiking with the group and I absolutely felt the difference between my fitness level and that of everyone else. Actually, Becky from our group was on par with me, so it was everyone else and then the two of us. It was disconcerting, and it gave me a sinking feeling in my stomach. Everyone else could just bound up these huge stone stairs, and I was struggling. Was I going to fail on the Inca Trail? Was I unable to hack it? Even with all my months of working out and preparing I was still going to fail miserably. I wasn't fit enough for the Inca Trail. Suddenly my mind went to all of the blog articles I had read about other people who had tried to hike the Inca Trail but failed after the first day. My over-preparation was again proving to be my undoing, as it was getting in my head.

I'm certain Miguel wanted me on the mini-hike to assess my hiking abilities, but also to give me a dose of the reality for what I was in for. Not more than I needed, but just the right amount of information.   On the way back down from our mini-hike, I was starting to panic. These stone steps were STEEP! They were hard to go up and down. I knew day two of the Inca Trail was almost entirely uphill, up to the highest point on the trail. Would it be like these steps? That steep, all day?! That dreadful thought, together with the blog stories of dismal failure going on repeat in my head...I was spiraling. I was starting to think I couldn't do it. So I caught up to Miguel and asked him if this was what day two would be like. I know he could hear the panic in my voice as I was fighting back the tears. Miguel's response was so kind. He said that yes, some of the steps on day two would be that steep—but not all of them. But then he uttered the phrase I would hear repeated from him many times over the next few days, "all things are possible on the Inca Trail. Do not think about day two yet. Think only about today." All things are possible on the Inca Trail. I wanted to believe that so badly. His words of advice, "think only about today" would also echo in my head throughout the trek.

But see, Miguel, I don't really do very well at thinking about only the moment, or the day in front of me. I like to PREPARE! I like to PLAN! (And I like to dwell and stew and fret and worry...) But here is where the key comes in. Preparation is one thing: preparing my body and having a sense of what I am getting myself into (like through the practice hike), those things are good. But over-preparation can be dangerous, particularly mental over-preparation. Well-meaning preparation can very quickly turn a corner into obsession and over-preparation and stewing. Miguel's strategy was to tackle only the obstacle right in front of me today, and leave the others for tomorrow. Don't waste energy worrying about tomorrow's obstacle; we need that energy today.

I wish I could say that I heard Miguel's words that afternoon in Ollantaytambo, and that I took them to heart and applied them immediately. But I didn't. I heard them, I wanted to believe, but instead I worried. I worried about the things I couldn't pack in my duffel bag. I worried about my lack of fitness. I worried about how everyone else was so much faster than me and how I would hold everyone back. The ONLY thing I can say is that I had enough sense in me to stop allowing myself to think about my fears of failing the trail, because at this point I had no choice. I was going to do it. So it took all of my strength to stop myself from thinking about any possibility of me failing to complete the hike. But I worried about everything else. And I began to feel nauseous with worry.

After the practice hike, we went to dinner as a group. All around me, the group was laughing and eating together, enjoying each other's company the night before we set out to tackle the Inca Trail. Everyone seemed so light-hearted. But not me. I was struggling to control my nausea. I knew I needed to eat to have strength for the hike (spoiler alert: this will be a recurring theme for pretty much the entire trip,) but I lacked any appetite. I got through dinner and went back to the hotel and spent much of the night in my bed, willing myself to sleep. I tried to keep Miguel's words in my head. I tried to remember that the day ahead of me was the "easy day" of the hike, and that's all I needed to think about. Enjoy the journey: this is supposed to be sort of fun, right? But the evil over-preparation was threatening to undo me.

So. Lesson two from the Inca Trail is an essential one for me. Preparation is good. It's important. It's essential. But over-preparation can be deadly. And with my propensity for preparation and planning, I need to be particularly vigilant against this. This is a lesson I desperately need to take with me beyond the Inca Trail. Yes, planning and preparation may be a method I use to manage my anxiety, but I need to be careful not to overdo it, and cause myself more hardship and anxiety in the long run. I must learn to be free sometimes and let things be as they will be. Little by little, I must learn to trust the universe more, and try to control less.

Chapter 4: We Are Not alone; Rely on our "Family," Whoever That May Be.

> *"The Universe provides abundantly when you are in a state of gratefulness."* -Wayne Dyer

Day one of the hike is the "easy day". I knew this because I read about it many, many times. (See chapter 2. And chapter 3. Moving on.) I knew it was the day with the least amount of elevation change. I knew it was the day to kind of try out hiking. Get our "hiking legs" (You know…kind of like sea legs?) So when we started hiking and the first thing we did was walk up a giant hill, and it was hard, I thought, "what is this madness?!? This is only the first few feet on the first day, it can't be this hard already!" But then it really did level out, just like they said, and it was fun! I liked it. My fears *started* to dissipate a bit. I saw Miguel along the trail and I said, "Hey! This is fun! Can you keep it flat like this the whole four days?! I would really love that." Miguel gave me a kind of knowing smile (maybe a slightly evil smile?) and chuckled a bit.

It was kind of "easy" except there wasn't any shade, and the sun was absolutely beating down on us. By the time we stopped for lunch after about 3 hours of hiking, I felt cooked. I had a hard time eating, but I did my best. I tried to rest a bit, but I just felt exhausted and overheated. And all too soon, the hike started back up. Still level for a bit, and then gradually we started going up. Not surprisingly, my speed started decreasing rapidly.

I had spent most of the first day walking with my friend Cindy. Cindy is infinitely more fit than I am. We have been friends and running partners for years, but whenever we run together, she most definitely has to run my pace, which is a good two or three minutes slower per mile than her own pace. So it was with the Inca Trail. Once the trail started going uphill, I kept having to stop and catch my breath…and Cindy kept waiting with me. She never complained, of course, but I felt terrible. I don't like to feel like I am holding someone back, but I definitely felt that way with her on day one. Between the relentless, burning, dehydrating sun, the increasing elevation, the pack on my back which wasn't exactly light, and the overarching doom and worry about how hard the next day would be, I was starting to panic. It was a much more difficult and exhausting day than I had anticipated. I tried to keep my mind steady and clear and thinking only about the trail in front of me at that moment. But I couldn't help thinking that if I was finding day one (the easy day) this difficult, how much more awful was the rest of the trail going to be? How was I ever going to survive day two?. By the time we staggered into camp, I was done. Super done. Over done.

It was about 5:30 PM when we got into camp that night. The porters had arrived hours earlier and set up our tents for us. They had a practice of applauding each time people made it into camp at the end of the day, which was sometimes annoying, and sometimes wonderful, and sometimes quite emotional. That day, since it was the first day and I wasn't expecting it…it was a little confusing. We were finally at camp and I was so exhausted and feeling so sick, but all these people were standing up and clapping and I was confused. As most of our group was there already, they had found their tents. Cindy and I quickly located ours, by the duffel bags which had been placed nicely inside, and I immediately crashed. I laid down, boots still on, feeling seriously nauseous and cold and miserable. I really wasn't interested in moving again, ever.

But darkness was coming quickly, and there were things that needed to be done while it was still light. The porters brought over a pan of warm water to wash up, I had to get my boots off and put on my camp shoes so my feet could breathe, I had to get my bed set up while there was still daylight. So many things I had to do. I did the best I could going through these tasks, but I was seriously doubting my ability to keep going. The nausea was overpowering me.

Nausea is like my kryptonite in life. Whenever anything happens to me, my body's first instinct is to feel like puking. Rarely do I actually vomit (a good thing) but it takes very very little for my body to start feeling like I might. Anytime I have a headache, or get the least bit nervous about something, the nausea appears. At one time in my life I went to a gastrointestinal specialist and had every test in the world done on me. In the end, they found nothing wrong with me and diagnosed the nausea as "psychosomatic" which I didn't love hearing. But I accept it, and I know it to be true. That does not make it any less real or any less miserable, however.

As darkness arrived at camp, roughly 6:00 PM, the temperature dramatically dropped. We were at a high enough elevation that the temperature would get down to near-freezing the first night and below freezing the second night. This was a shock to my body, which was overheated and now a little bit sunburned from the hike that day. To go from hot and sunburnt to now freezing cold…that was another cause for my body to react with nausea. I was not doing well.

Miguel called the 15 of us hiking together a family. The term was nice enough at first—who doesn't love to be part of a family? But as the hike went on, the term became more and more special. We were hiking together. Striving to reach mountaintops together. We were surviving together, eating together, sleeping very closely together, sharing this experience of a lifetime together. Very quickly we got to know the others in our family and even if their idiosyncrasies annoyed me, they were still family and I cherished them.

In the family were the four of us girls, a 4-person actual family from DC (mother, father, and two sons, ages 18 and 20), a 30ish couple from England, 2 20-something girls from Canada, and 3 people in their very early 20s each travelling alone, from Australia, New Zealand, and Norway. Several of the young people (basically that's what I considered everyone besides the four of us and the DC family) were hiking the Inca Trail as part of a larger 2 month trip around South America. So…these kids were tough. They had been away from home for a long time and had been traveling through Brazil, Argentina and Bolivia before they even got to Perú. They were really fun people to talk to and get to know a bit; I was glad to be sharing this 4 day journey with them. I loved the idea of being a family together with all of them, with Miguel, Yossep and Saul taking care of us all.

Miguel gathered the family for dinner that night and asked how the first day went. Most people were positive and happy. Kellie was positively glowing; she was in her element. The scenery was beautiful, the Incan ruins we saw that day were spectacular, the mountain vistas were indescribable: it really was a great day. The only problem was…I was miserable. I KNEW my nausea was a lie. I knew it was a psychosomatic reaction inside my head. But it was terribly hard to convince my body of that.

Miguel saw me not eating and got concerned. Very, very slowly, mind over matter, I tried desperately to eat the rice and chicken at least, if not the vegetables. I sat there until the meal was cold, still forcing myself to put food in my mouth, chew, and swallow. But in the end, I was not able to eat much. Miguel gave the family the instructions about the next day (again, telling us only the pieces of information we needed for that moment) and it sounded terrifying. We were supposed to be ascending for four or five hours, and I knew it would be longer for me since I went so slowly. How could I even consider climbing up for more than five hours, if I couldn't eat any food? I knew I needed energy to hike. That scared me even more.

We went to bed shortly after dinner, even though it was probably only 7:30 or 8:00 PM. Our wakeup call the next morning would be at 5:00 AM, so we needed to go to bed early. Sleep was elusive. My body decided it needed to go to the bathroom roughly 5,000 times that night, every half hour. I theorized that the body prioritizes systems, and I don't think my kidney/urinary system was a priority during the day while hiking. I didn't go to the bathroom at all during the day, despite drinking roughly 4 liters of water during the hike. But once night fell and I laid down in my sleeping bag, my kidneys woke up and I started going to the bathroom every half hour. Which would have been annoying on a regular night. Here, I was wrapped in as many layers as possible, wearing my hat and gloves, zipped up in my sleeping bag and inside my tent and it was a serious pain to keep getting up.

Meanwhile, the nausea raged on. And my mind continued to stew and worry about the long climb I had ahead of me on day two. I kept willing myself to sleep, knowing my body needed to recharge for the horrible day ahead of me. My body kept responding with nausea. By the time our 5:00 wakeup call hit, I had only a few hours of sleep and my body was in full revolt. As I got dressed and ready for the hike, I was overwhelmingly scared of what lay ahead of me that day.

Cindy and I went down to the breakfast tent. I had told her that I was not planning to hike with her that day. I would stay at the back and walk with Becky. I was feeling so sick, and I didn't want to hold Cindy back. Cindy and Kellie were much speedier anyway, so it made sense for the two of them to team up closer to the front of the pack and for Becky and I to team up at the back. Down at breakfast, I struggled once again to eat anything. The food looked delicious—we had pancakes that morning and the chefs had decorated the plates with animals made out of some kind of honey sauce. Once again, I slowly forced myself to eat bites, each time my mind willing my mouth to swallow the food, even though my body thought it wanted to throw it up. Miguel was concerned, assuming I was exhibiting signs of altitude sickness. As it was, another girl in our group was dealing with full-on altitude sickness and she had been up all night vomiting. I assured Miguel that this was just my body's typical response. I was nauseous, but not really sick. Miguel seemed skeptical and still worried.

So at breakfast on the morning of the second day, I was trying every mind-over-matter technique I had to force myself to eat something since I had the hike of my life ahead of me. The parents of the DC family casually said to me, "Hey, we have a medicine kit we brought with us and we think there might be some anti-nausea medication in there. Would you be interested?" Would. I. Be. INTERESTED?!? Are you kidding me?!? They told me that they had been given this medicine kit before a trip abroad with an employer and on a whim, they had decided to bring it with them on the Inca Trail, "just in case." (My mind immediately went to all of the items that I couldn't bring into my duffel bag because they were too heavy, and how is it that this family had the foresight and the DUFFEL BAG WEIGHT left to bring any "just in case" items?! That thought, however, was not helpful, so I stuffed it out of my mind.) I followed them up to their bag. He cracked open the medicine kit and sure enough, there was some prescription anti-nausea medication, Zofran. I knew it well because I had been prescribed it before by my gastrointestinal doctor. I just looked up at these family members and said, "Are you serious? I can have this?" They assured me that it was fine and they were happy to help. The instructions were to take one pill every six hours, so he gave me three pills for the day.

Shortly after that, we had our backpacks strapped on our backs and our hiking poles in our hands, and I began the long, slow ascent toward the highest point on the trail. We started hiking by 6:30 AM. It was slow, trudging, step by step, stopping to catch my breath often. The rest of the family (especially the young kids) were long gone ahead of me. Becky and I got to the first stopping place at about 7:30 AM, about the time that the rest of the family were beginning to move out. But I had to share my exciting news with the DC family (and the whole family) that I was hungry! I was actually hungry! For the first time since starting the Inca Trail, I was hungry. Which meant my nausea was being kept at bay by the medication. I was never so excited to take off my backpack and dig inside for a snack. It was wonderful. I thought to myself, "I am going to be okay. This is going to be okay. This day is going to be hard. It will be hell. But I am going to do it. I am going to be okay."

And so, on the morning of day two, the Inca Trail taught me that I am not alone. I need to rely on my family…whatever family the universe gives me. For those four days, my family consisted of 14 other travelers from across the globe, three Peruvian guides, and a host of porters (more on them later). But the very real truth is that I could not have survived the Inca Trail without leaning on my family. Whatever providence made that DC family pack that medicine kit, it saved my life. I will forever be grateful to them. I am also grateful for the lesson (another one I might need to relearn several times in life) that I can't do it all on my own. I need people. I need the people that have been put into my life. I need to trust them and rely on them and be grateful for them. This isn't a sign of weakness, to need my family members. It's a sign that I am a human being, connected to the universe and to my fellow human beings who are on this journey through life with me. I may not be able to do it all on my own, but I can trust and rely on the family and the people in my life that have been given to me. Thank you, Inca Trail, for teaching me this lesson.

Chapter 5: Go Your Own Pace

"If a man does not keep pace with his companions, perhaps it is because he hears a different drummer. Let him step to the music which he hears, however measured or far away. It is not important that he should mature as soon as an appletree or an oak. Shall he turn his spring into summer?" –Henry David Thoreau, Walden

Logic would suggest that going slow and steady would be a good way for anyone to complete the Inca Trail. It worked for the tortoise; wouldn't it work for everyone else? And slow and steady isn't incorrect, but the more exact lesson I learned on the trail was to go at my pace. Exactly at my pace, not faster or slower to accommodate any other hiker. On day two, when we set out to begin the hours-long, seemingly impossible continuous climb toward the highest point on the trail, I was determined to stay at the back of the pack with Becky and Saul, the guide who was bringing up the rear that day. And initially, I did stay with them, but Saul pretty quickly gathered that my hiking rhythm was *ever so slightly* faster than Becky's, and he stressed to me that I needed to go my own pace. The anti-nausea meds were kicking in and I felt a sense of energy (and hunger!) that I hadn't felt in hours and I didn't know how long it would last, so I took his advice. I made sure Becky was fine if I went a bit ahead and she assured me again that I needed to go my own pace, just as she needed to go hers.

I spent many hours that day hiking alone, at my own pace. I saw the group briefly at the first resting point, but Miguel had a new plan that day. While on day one he used the rest times as a way to gather the group together, so that the back-of-the-pack people could catch up with the rest of the family, Miguel was not doing that on the second day. Or perhaps he was, to an extent, but they were not waiting for Becky and me. Which was a little sad, but okay. Just as I needed to go my pace, they needed to go theirs, and I did not want to feel like I was holding anyone back.

Later that day when I got to camp (finally) and saw Kellie and Cindy, they also said they had spent most of their day hiking alone, each at their own pace. It wasn't just Saul preaching this advice; Miguel and Yossep were saying the same thing, encouraging each member of the family to go at their own individual pace. I thought I was the different one, hiking alone most of the day, and I had been kind of grumpy about that, and the whole "go your own pace" advice, thinking "my pace" means "I'm alone." But it turns out that everyone's pace meant that for that time, when we were climbing and climbing, everyone was walking alone.

And yet, we weren't. We were all walking the same path. I didn't see my sister that day at all, from the moment we left camp at 6:30 AM until the moment I reached camp again in the late afternoon. And yet my feet were tracing her footsteps up the mountain. And her feet were tracing someone else's footprints. And all of us were tracing the footprints of the people who had hiked the day before, and the day before that, and last year, and 10 years ago. Oh yeah, and 500 years ago when it was the Incas traveling this trail, carrying their emperor up high on a litter.

The guides were so insistent to us that we go our own pace, because they understood that this was the only way we could survive. If we pushed too hard to go too fast to keep up with people whose pace was faster than ours, we would burn out and run out of energy and mental strength before we got to the top. This is simple but essential advice for life outside the Inca Trail too. We are each on our own journey. We may be moving faster than some along the journey, and slower than others, but we each need the freedom and grace to move at our own pace. We can't pressure ourselves or anyone else to move at a faster pace than we can go. Nor can we artificially hold ourselves up from progressing along our journey when we are ready to do so. We journey with others and we see them along the way. When we come home for the night, we step in from our journey and reconnect with our family, loved ones, and fellow travelers. We catch up, share our individual perspectives from the day's journey.

We reconnect and relax and rest together. And then the next day, we get up and keep moving at our own pace once again. So it was on the Inca Trail, so it should be for the rest of our journey in life.

Chapter 6: Keep Moving Forward

"The only thing a person can ever really do is keep moving forward. Take that big leap forward without hesitation, without once looking back. Simply forget the past and forge toward the future." -Alyson Noel

The Inca Trail is no joke. Since I have been back, when people ask me about it, I always say it is the single most difficult thing I have ever experienced in my life. Difficult physically, emotionally, mentally, and spiritually. Now that I have been back for a little while…I still think that is an accurate statement, albeit perhaps a tiny bit hyperbolic.

I've done hard things in my life. Many of them, as I explained in the introduction to this book, have happened within the last several years. I faced daunting new positions at work, navigating a divorce and protecting two young children through that process (as much as possible), and then I experienced the indescribable trauma of witnessing the sudden and unexpected death of the man I loved. So how, then, could I say that the Inca Trail was the HARDEST thing I've had to do? Isn't that a little bit silly?

I think what I mean is that the Inca Trail was hard on absolutely every level. Physically, it was the hardest thing I've ever done. Before I hiked the trail, I had run/walked two half-marathons. I had kept moving, as fast as I could, for three hours. That was hard, but at the end of the three hours, I went home to my house to put ice on my knees, take Advil, eat normal food, and then sleep in my bed. But the Inca Trail, at the end of three hours of intense exercise, I had to keep going. And going. And going. After the first day of seven or eight hours of hiking, I didn't get my own bed. Or any bed, for that matter. I got a sleeping bag on the hard ground, in a freezing cold tent. And the next day, I got the hardest hike of my life. I couldn't rely on just physical strength to keep going, because my body wanted to be done long before the end of the first day. I had to dig down deep into emotional strength to keep going. I had to rely on my spiritual strength, when each breath was a prayer to God to give me the next breath.

The second day was grueling. I was inching forward, step by step, but it was slow going. The uphill climb was relentless. I would peer around each switchback corner hoping that the road ahead might be flat for a little bit, but each time I was greeted with more stairs up. I had two strategies I would employ in my mind to help me cope. Sometimes I would look to a landmark up ahead (a bush or a tree) and try to keep walking until I reached the landmark. But mostly, I counted steps. First I tried to get 50 steps in before stopping to catch my breath and lower my heart rate. Then it was 45…then 40…and then 35. I tried not to do less than 35 steps, though I confess sometimes I did.

The step counting method did a couple things: one, it broke the relentless climb down into something manageable, and provided a different perspective of the amazing scenery, each 35 steps. More importantly, it filled my head with something. My mind was preoccupied with counting my steps, so I didn't have room in my brain to think about how tired I was, or how much my legs or my lungs hurt, or how loudly my pulse was beating in my head. I couldn't think about how long it was taking to get to the top, or how far behind the group we were, or how late it would be by the time we got to camp, or any number of other thoughts that wanted to take up residence in my mind. It was an emotionally and mentally exhausting hike because all of my brain power was devoted to keeping those thoughts out. All I could do was count steps, and keep moving forward.

Keep moving forward became a bit of a battle cry for my hike, especially during day two when the climb was so arduous. During the last couple hours toward the highest point of the hike, Becky and I were climbing together. Yes, it's important to go your own pace, but in that portion of the climb, I needed the company. I needed my teammate on this part of the trek, and so our paces joined up. And we both needed our guide Saul who quietly, kindly, pushed us up and over that mountain. Sometimes he would hang back behind us a bit and let us move forward on our own. As we neared the top and the steps got steeper and the air got thinner and we were gasping for breath, Saul moved in front of us, mentally pulling us up the mountain, willing us to go forward. Saul would ask how we were doing and I would answer with the battle cry, "Always forward, siempre adelante!"

One thing that keeps the Inca Trail is interesting is the fact that there is no good escape route. During the first day, we hiked past a couple of really tiny villages and I suppose if someone were hurt or unable to continue on the hike, something could possibly be worked out with a horse or donkey from one of the villages. But once we got to a certain point on day two, it was basically a point of no return. It was too far to turn around, so we simply had to keep going to Machu Picchu, whether on our own power or (if we were severely hurt), on the back of a porter. So "always forward" was a bit of a funny battle cry because at that point, there was no choice but to go forward. And since there was NO POSSIBLE WAY I was going to give up and ask a porter to carry me, I had no choice but to propel myself forward.

Hiking the Inca Trail brought the "keep moving forward" mantra to life in a very real way. This journey was not metaphorical, as so many of our journeys are. This was a physical journey where we had to literally keep moving forward. But this lesson from the trail is absolutely applicable. Whatever life throws at us, we have two choices. We can remain stationary and refuse to grow and change and live...or we can keep moving forward, toward the next landmark, taking breaks as often as we need to catch our breath. We move forward at our own pace, but we keep moving forward.

The man I loved died on a Friday afternoon. I spent that weekend in a daze, as family members moved around me. I was in shock; I didn't know what to do about anything. I remember waking up in the morning on Sunday and feeling hungry, but I was absolutely powerless to do anything about the hunger. I didn't know how to fix it. I crawled into the hall outside the rooms where my mom and my sister were sleeping, and I literally crumpled into a ball on the floor. I heard myself cry out (to my sleeping family members), "Will somebody tell me what to eat?!" My mom and my sister, gifts of God to me, jumped to attention and said "Of course!" They started making all kinds of food until there was something in front of me that I was able to eat.

I wanted to stay curled into a ball; I wanted to give up. The pain was unspeakable and I didn't know how I could continue. But I had no choice. The following day was Monday, and it was the first day of school. My children were six and eight, entering first and fourth grade. I was supposed to be at the bus stop to take pictures and see them off for their first day. All my body wanted to do was curl up into a ball and die with Ron, but I couldn't do that to my children. For them, I had to keep moving forward. Inching along at times, but...siempre adelante.

The Inca Trail reminded me of this lesson. It reminded me of how it feels to rely on God for each breath, and when each step forward feels like a victory.

Our journey is not always this difficult, but even when it is, we must keep moving forward. Even if it's only inching forward very slowly, that is still progress.

Chapter 7: Put your Poles on the Next Step

"The forest did not tolerate frailty of body or mind. Show your weakness, and it would consume you without hesitation." -Tahir Shah, <u>House of the Tiger King: The Quest for a Lost City</u>

I had never hiked with poles before the Inca Trail. I wasn't sure how they worked, but everything I read (in my EXTENSIVE preparation) told me to hike with two poles. It wasn't an option: they said I would need them, period. We were skeptical at first, especially Kellie. She was like, "Why am I carrying these useless sticks around?" The flat part at the beginning of the trail was a bit of a trick like that. But as soon as we started going up in altitude, I began to understand. It took some time to get coordinated and figure out how to use them, but I soon learned to put my poles ahead of me and transfer my weight through my hands onto the poles. They became even more indispensable when we were going down. The stairs on the Inca Trail were SERIOUSLY steep and having the poles to lean on and gain traction were very important. They saved my knees.

So on day two, when we were continuously going up, and I was learning to go my own pace, and remembering what it felt like to keep moving forward, the trail also taught me to put my poles on the next step. I would take my 35 steps and then rest for as long as it took for my heart to stop racing and my breathing to return to something resembling a normal rate. But each time at the end of those rests, I had to start up again. I knew this, of course, because there was no choice but to (wait for it) keep going forward. But my body was having trouble getting this message sometimes, and it became harder and harder to convince my feet to keep going after a rest.

So I learned to rest my poles on the step in front of me. It was a simple act, but it was a message to my body: "Rest up a minute, but don't get too comfortable because this is where we are headed next." My body needed that subtle direction, because (if I let myself realize it) I was exhausted. Especially on day two, when I hadn't slept the night before or eaten anything at dinner and breakfast. My body wanted to give up and give in, but my poles were on the next step, ready to go as soon as my body caught up.

I looked back and saw that there had been times before hiking the Inca Trail when I learned to put my proverbial poles on the next step, to point myself in the direction of where I was headed. After Ron died, and I managed to wake up and see my kids off to the bus stop that Monday morning, my motherhood role wasn't complete. That night I would have the kids at my house for the first night since his death. Not only that, but it was the first day of school and our tradition was to get pizza and go to the park after school to celebrate getting through the day. I had managed to find the strength to meet them at the bus stop and take their pictures, but once they were on the bus, I couldn't just give up. I put my poles on the next step, and prepared for the evening with the kids. I asked my friend/next-door-neighbor to help me because I didn't think I could do it alone. And together, we went to pick up the kids and get pizza and play at the park. And then, once the kids were in bed for the night and I had made it though, I again put my poles on the next step and prepared for what was ahead of me for the next day.

I think this lesson is particularly interesting when I think about what hiking poles are. They are assistants, there to make hiking easier. We don't need hiking poles for normal everyday walking. I can go up and down stairs a million times during the day without the assistance of any poles. But when we are hiking—especially strenuous, multiple-day hikes—poles become essential, which is another lesson in and of itself. It's one more reminder that when we are doing hard things, we can't expect to stand on our own two feet all the time. EVERYONE uses hiking poles. Even our guides carried poles with them. Miguel had hiked the Inca Trail more than 350 times, and he still used hiking poles, because it is a HARD hike, and poles are essential.

So, we can't feel bad when we need assistance (or assistive gear) in life. We should ask for and accept that assistance and not feel the least amount of guilt for it. And there may be times when the going is so rough, and it is so much mind-over-matter, that we may find it helpful to rest our poles on the next step, silently willing our body to move in that direction once it has rested. Step by step, we will make it through this journey called life.

Chapter 8: Tears—Expect Them, and Don't Be Afraid of Them

"No one ever told me that grief felt so like fear."
-C.S. Lewis, A Grief Observed

So…I've explained that hiking the Inca Trail is more than just a hike—it's intensely physical, as well as emotionally and mentally exhausting. But there was also an intense spiritual component to the hike, at least for me. I was there with three other women, to celebrate my impending 40th birthday. I was there, in part, to prove to myself that even at nearly 40, I could still do super hard things. I could do anything I put my mind to, despite my age. I was also of the belief that God had put the four of us on that trip at that exact point in time for specific reasons. We each had our burdens to bear, our "stuff" that we were going through at that time. Kellie, Becky, and Cindy have their own stories and they are not mine to tell. But nevertheless, I was convinced that God had been working in all four of us and placed us each on that mountain, at that time, to do the work God wanted to do in our lives. That's heavy stuff.

The night before we left Cusco city, I gathered the four of us together and gave everyone (myself included) a silver necklace with two pendants. One was a small silver circle with jagged mountains inside, which (unbeknownst to me when I bought them) look strikingly like Huayna Picchu, the tall mountain that is the backdrop to the Machu Picchu citadel. The other pendant said, "Adventure awaits," which more or less summed up my thoughts for us about our experience in Perú. I believe that God had a plan for each of us to be on this trip, to do some work in our lives, and for us to leave the mountain hopefully free of some of our baggage, ready to embrace the future. The great adventure, whatever that is for each of us, was awaiting, just on the other side of Machu Picchu.

Perhaps because my mind was open and expecting to see God on this trip, my emotions were more raw and open also. Perhaps it's just that it was impossible NOT to see God on this hike. Each time I looked up from the trail, I was surrounded by the most beautiful views I had ever seen in my life. There were no cars, no roads, and no noise to distract. Just the indescribable beauty of this planet. At times I was surrounded by trees and rocks with the stream trickling beside the trail; other times (when we got above the tree line) there were only small shrubs and grasses. We could look across the valley and see the mountains surrounding us and the alpacas grazing high on the mountainsides; the beauty of all of that took my breath away. (Whatever breath I had left, after the altitude took its share.) There were ponds high up in the mountains with the clearest water I have ever seen. On the third day we descended into the cloud forest and found ourselves in the high jungle, introducing a new intense beauty, entirely different than what we saw the first two days. Hummingbirds, orchids, tropical flowers, vines and greenery were everywhere. There really aren't words to describe how beautiful it all was. And there I was, in the midst of it, so privileged to be able to travel this ancient trail and see this beautiful part of the planet. I was walking on a road that had been constructed some 500-600 years before, and had been used only by Inca royalty. As it is now, only 500 humans are allowed on the trail each day. Only a very tiny fraction of the population on this planet will ever be able to walk on this trail, and I got to be one of them.

Now THAT'S heavy stuff.

And so, with all of that as the backdrop in my mind every day, it's not a surprise that I was feeling emotional. When I was hiking uphill, I was focused. I had to keep my mind focused on counting stairs or marking my progress somehow, so there wasn't room in my head for negative thoughts. That tended to keep the emotions locked away, too. But when I would make it to a resting point, and I took a moment to realize and appreciate what my body was doing, and how privileged I was to be in this sacred place, there was no holding back the tears. That moment on day two when I finally made it to the top of Dead Woman's Pass, there were a few tears. I refused to let myself feel everything fully at that point, though, because I knew I still had hours of hiking left to do that day. But despite my attempts at stoicism, I couldn't stop all the tears from falling. I had made it to the highest point. Arguably the hardest part of the hike was behind me. I had done it. By the grace of God alone, I had done it. Despite feeling so ill the night before, I had gotten myself to the top of Dead Woman's Pass, and I was alive. As Becky, Saul, and I celebrated that moment at the top of the mountain, all three of us had tears in our eyes. We experienced the emotion of that moment together and it was beautiful.

I didn't allow myself to rest in that moment for long. There were still hours to go—maybe three more hours left to hike that day, but this time downhill. I had a limited amount of water in my backpack and I was concerned about that. I needed to keep moving. Saul gave us a quick lesson in how to use our poles to go down the millions of stairs on the Inca Trail, and we were off. Once again, I moved at my own pace, slightly faster than Becky and Saul, so I soon found myself alone on the trail. I just kept moving forward. The sun was beating down and I was exhausted. My energy was low, but I couldn't allow myself to get complacent. Even the parts of the path that didn't have stairs were still difficult. The trail was a steady decline with large rocks making a rough-hewn cobblestone path. Tripping and falling was a very real concern and I was not interested in cracking my head open on a rock in the middle of nowhere. So I had to keep my mind fully engaged. About two hours after starting the descent, my fears were realized and my water ran out. Now, I could have stayed put and waited for Saul and Becky to catch up; I knew Saul had extra water in his pack that he would have given me, and they likely weren't that far behind. But I didn't think about that, nor did I know how far behind me they were. So I kept going as quickly as possible, and 45 minutes after my water ran out, I finally got to camp.

Each day the porters would pack up camp and run ahead of our group, making their way to the next night's camp. Once there, they set up all the tents, collected water and boiled it to make it safe for us, and started cooking. One porter remained stationed on the trail with our purple G Adventures flag. He would make sure that all of the group came in and didn't miss the camp turn off.

He would then signal to all of the other porters that another hiker had completed the trail for the day and they would all stand and applaud. At some points the porters' praise and celebration felt superfluous, almost embarrassing. These men ran along the trail carrying HUMOUNGOUS packs and made it much much quicker than me. Why do I deserve applause for crawling along the trail at my pathetic snail's pace? But I confess at the end of the second day of hiking…at the end of the hardest hike of my entire life…the sound of their applause was wonderful.

When I saw that porter there with the purple flag and I knew I had made it to camp where I could get more water and stop hiking, and I knew I had gotten through the hardest day on the trail and survived, I could no longer hold back: the floodgates of emotion were forced open. I began to sob. I walked the last bit, through the crowd of porters clapping, with tears streaming down my face. The rest of "the family" (as Miguel calls our group) were all there and had eaten already, (the only day that Miguel allowed the family to eat before we were all present and accounted for) so they were all anxious to see Becky and me arrive safely too. They heard the porters' applause when I arrived and came out of their tents to celebrate with them. This made me cry harder, knowing that these wonderful people who had been strangers just days before were now joining with me, sharing in my joy upon completing the hardest day. And then at end of the line was Miguel, who stood there waiting for me, his arms outstretched, ready to welcome me to camp.

It reminded me of the parable in the Bible of the prodigal son. In that parable, a son asks for his inheritance while his father is still alive, and once he receives it, he leaves and proceeds to squander his fortune on hedonism. Despite the pain his father feels at this betrayal, he loves and misses his beloved son. Every day the father stands at the end of the lane, looking up the road, watching and waiting and hoping for the young man's return. When the son finally does return (because he is out of money) the father is overjoyed to have his son back and there is a great celebration. Naturally in this biblical parable, the father is a picture of God who always welcomes us with open arms and love, no matter what we have done. When I saw Miguel there with his arms open wide, he reminded me of the father (that is, God) in that parable. Not that I had done anything wrong, particularly, but that he was still there, watching and waiting, not resting until Becky and I were back in the fold.

So in my already emotional state, when I saw Miguel standing there with his arms wide open, welcoming me, seeming like God incarnate right there in the mountains of Perú, I lost it. I clung to Miguel and just sobbed and sobbed, the ugliest cry I had. Miguel held me and told me how proud he was of me. He told me I had made it, and I had done a good job. All of which, naturally, made me cry even harder. Then I turned around and saw Kellie and Cindy, and I found I could still cry harder. They were tears of joy for making it through the hardest day, gratitude to Saul and Miguel for guiding us, gratitude to God for giving me enough breath for each step, maybe tears of fear of what was still to come, tears of awe at the beauty all around me, and a million other reasons. I cried tears of missing my children and loved ones back home, and also tears of missing my loved ones who had passed on before me. I cried tears of grief for Ron, and thought how Miguel's words sounded like the voice of Ron. It was like confirmation that Ron was watching over me somehow, that he could see this difficult feat I had accomplished, as if he had borrowed Miguel so that he could communicate those words to me to tell me how proud he was of me, and that I had done well.

In short, I was an emotional mess. Every dam I had placed on the river of my emotions earlier that day in order to get through the hike was completely flooded. And once those feelings were out, it seems I couldn't stop them. During days three and four of the hike, I cried often. Sometimes they were happy tears; many times they were not. But at all times, my emotions were raw and right at the surface.

If we want to grow and change and really live, it will be hard. We were never promised an easy road in this life. So when we fully embrace those hard things, it will be emotional. I believe one of the reasons I was placed on the Inca Trail was to process some of my grief from Ron's passing. When Ron died, I made the conscious choice to continue living, which included remaining open to new love. And in fact, I have fallen in love with a wonderful, kind, and incredibly strong man and we are dreaming and planning for our future together. I know that is right and good, and I know that Ron would not want me to have effectively died with him. I know that. And yet, it still feels a little unfair sometimes. Unfair that I should get to continue on and find new happiness, while his life got cut tragically short. I didn't know how, but I was hoping that somehow on the Inca Trail, I could get some measure of...*something.* Not closure, because grief never ends. I didn't know what I was looking for, but I trusted that God would reveal it when it was time.

At the end of the hike on day two, when Miguel waited for me with open arms, seeming like God hugging the prodigal son, and he told me he was proud of me...in my mind I heard Ron saying that. It was Ron telling me he was proud of me for getting through that hike, but also proud of me for continuing to live. For doing the hard things to take care of my children, and for taking the supreme risk at love again. It was as if Ron, through the voice of Miguel, was giving me his blessing for the path my life was taking. For the adventure that awaited, on the other side of Machu Picchu.

And so, the Inca Trail taught me to embrace the tears in life. They wash our emotional wounds and they are healing. Tears should be embraced, not feared.

Chapter 9: Breathe Out the Bad Stuff That's No Longer Needed.

"Learn how to exhale, the inhale will take care of itself." -Carla Melucci Ardito

OK! Last chapter was a little too deep and emotional, so this chapter, we shall be a bit more practical to give the deep emotional stuff a small rest. Focusing on our exhaling breath was a basic piece of advice that the guides gave us on the trail. Perhaps I should have known this, or come across this wisdom elsewhere in my life but I never really thought about it this way before. When we were hiking uphill, we were typically out of breath. Because the inclines were steep and grueling, and also because of the high elevation and thin air. So there was a lot of huffing and puffing all the time. It was pretty annoying and I just felt pathetically out of shape most of the time.

The guides saw our labored breathing as we were ascending, which I'm certain is normal with Inca Trail hikers who are unaccustomed to the altitude, so they gave us some breathing advice. They recommended we focus only on exhaling the air from our lungs; then the lungs would naturally inhale all on their own. I'm not sure why this exercise made such a difference, but it actually worked. Each time I had to stop to catch my breath, I would concentrate on the exhale and picture getting all the old, bad air out of my lungs. I wouldn't even think about the inhale, which just sort of happened anyway. Maybe it was a crazy mind trick, but I really feel like focusing on just the exhale helped relax me and get my heartrate lowered and my breathing under control more quickly, so that I could keep going.

It occurred to me that this principle could be applied to life as well. Perhaps I need to focus more on exhaling the bad stuff in my life that is no longer needed, that no longer serves me. I thought of how freeing it feels to pare down my wardrobe to get rid of clothes that I haven't worn in years. How much more liberating would it be to let go of some of the emotional baggage that is no longer serving me? There are (were?) people in my life who wounded me and then moved on; now our friendships are no longer what they were. Why, then, do I continue to follow them on social media? Why do I watch their lives playing out from afar and continue feeling the ache and pain each time? How would it feel to breathe out those feelings of hurt and pain, and fully exhale those people from my life and my attention? Then, perhaps, I could trust my lungs to do the work on their own to fill up that space in my life and in my heart with good things, good relationships that feed my soul.

Chapter 10: Sometimes You Need a Hug

"I have learned that there is more power in a good strong hug than in a thousand meaningful words."
-Ann Hood

If I haven't emphasized this enough to make you all sick yet, let me say it again: hiking the Inca Trail was a profoundly emotional experience for me. I did my best to keep it inside. Sometimes because I wanted to, sometimes (like on the second day when we were hiking up to Dead Woman's Pass) it was because I *had* to keep it in just to survive. But the Inca Trail had other plans for me, and would not allow me to remain stoic for long.

Somewhere along the way—after the day two cryfest that I described a couple chapters ago, probably—I decided that sometimes, you just need a hug. And that's okay. Maybe I forget that too often. Perhaps in my efforts to be Supermom and a good employee and a good friend and a good partner and to do it all independently, without any help from anyone…perhaps I forget sometimes that I can't do everything perfectly all the time. Trying to do that is really, really hard. And sometimes, when we are doing hard things, getting a hug from someone makes all the difference in the world.

There were times on the trail when I felt shaky and sick and I wasn't sure how I could continue on to the finish. But then I would get a hug from Saul or Miguel or Kellie or Cindy or another family member and it gave me strength to keep moving forward. Or when I was on the beach that day when Ron died, watching the lifeguards and EMTs performing CPR on the man I loved, and a woman I didn't even know came and put her arm around me. She was at the beach on vacation, but she explained she was an ER nurse and she wanted to help me. This woman was a calming presence to me at a time when I was all alone and the world was spinning out of control. She gently turned me away so that I couldn't see the technicians working on Ron, but she calmly and clearly explained to me what they were doing. She answered my questions to the best of her ability and held me tight when there was no good answer that she could give me. When it was time, she walked me to the passenger door of the ambulance, handed me my bag, and hugged me tightly before saying goodbye.

Sometimes, we just really need a hug. And that's okay to admit.

Chapter 11: Trust the Guides in Your Life Who Have Been There, Done That. Follow Their Advice Implicitly.

"Somewhere between the bottom of the climb and the summit is the answer to the mystery why we climb." -Greg Child

So, I'm generally an independent person. Ok, that's a pretty good understatement. The truth is, from a very young age, I've just learned to sort of...take care of myself. If I have a need or a want, I meet that need myself and I don't like to rely on anyone else to do it for me. I'm not good with accepting help or feeling like I am not capable of doing something on my own.

I knew that sort of mindset would be a problem on the Inca Trail. No matter how much I read and prepared ahead of time, I was still going to be doing something that was juuuuuust on the edge of my comfort zone and capability. Rationally, I knew I would need to listen to and rely on the guides leading the group. This was made abundantly clear to me when Miguel took us on the short "practice hike" in Ollantaytambo, the afternoon before starting on the Inca Trail. Just that tiny hike itself got me freaked out about how difficult the Inca Trail would be for me, and how far behind everyone else I was going to be and I was starting to get very anxious.

When I confessed my anxiety to Miguel and started to ask him about the second day of the hike, his answer to me was twofold. First, he told me to not think so far ahead. Do not worry about day two yet, think only about the day in front of me. Day one is the easy day, think only about that. He also told me, "There are no worries, okay? Because there are **three Inca Warriors** on the Inca Trail." Each time he said this (and it was often) he emphasized, "**THREE Inca Warriors.**" G Adventures calls the guides on the Inca Trail "Inca

Warriors," and after spending four days with them, I can absolutely see why.

But at the time, I thought it was kind of odd for him to say…that's supposed to reassure me? I'm worried about getting through this hike alive, and actually making it to the top of Dead Woman's Pass without being a dead woman, and his response to me is that there are three guides in our group?! WHO CARES how many guides there are? Are they going to carry me over the mountain?!

No, obviously, the guides didn't carry me over the mountain. But I soon realized how important they were in my journey along the trail. Miguel told us he had hiked the Inca Trail over 350 times, as both a porter and a guide. He knew the trail very well, and he knew how it affected people. He knew where the tough places would be and how best to help reluctant hikers. He couldn't do the hike for me, but I felt a lot safer knowing I had someone so experienced and knowledgeable going with me and making sure I was safe. I also came to understand the benefit of having three guides for our large group. It meant there was always one guide in the lead, one at the end, and another filtering through the middle. It also meant we were better able to go our own (slow) pace without worrying about holding the rest of the group up. In smaller groups with only one guide, the group would have to stay together more. The team would start up and the guide would tell them where to gather to meet up. The faster people could go as fast as they wanted, but then they would need to stop and wait for the rest of their team. In our group, because there were three guides, Becky and I could go our own slow pace and the others would not need to wait for us to catch up each time. This was a huge comfort to us. Feeling slow and pathetic is one thing, but knowing that my slow pace was holding up others and making their hike more difficult and exhausting would be much worse.

I didn't understand at first why Miguel was trying to encourage and reassure me by telling me there would be three guides for our group, but once on the trail, it made perfect sense. On the second day of the hike, Saul was stationed at the back of the group. For the last couple hours of hiking toward the highest point, Becky and I were together and Saul was our constant cheerleader.

Near the end he walked in front of us and it was like he was psychologically pulling us up to the top. He was quiet when we were doing well, he told jokes when it looked like we were drooping and at all times he encouraged us and instilled us with confidence.

On the third day of hiking, we started with a few hours of climbing uphill, toward the second highest point in the trail. Once again, Miguel decided not to hold up the entire group for Becky and me to catch up, which was PERFECTLY FINE with us. However, on that day of the hike, we passed by a lot of Inca ruins. Since Becky and I were not keeping up with the rest of the group, we missed out on the guides teaching us about the ancient site. But in the beginning of day three, Yossep was stationed back with us and he gave us a private tour of the ruins. He even took some of the high mountain grasses and showed us how the Incas would braid them together to make a quipu rope, which was a method of communication for the ancient Incas. Because there were three Inca Warriors on our trek with us, Becky and I didn't miss out on any information, and we weren't anxious about keeping up with the rest of the group.

Most importantly, having a guide with us at the back of the pack all the time made me feel safe. Some parts of the trail were a bit treacherous, especially for me (with my fear of heights). There were some places where the trail clung to the side of a cliff. In actuality, there was plenty of room to hike, but it scared me. All I had to do was let out a little yelp and Saul or Yossep came running to hold my hand and walk next to me on the cliffside. Also, while the uphill parts of the trail were the hardest physically, the downhill segments were the most technically challenging and frightening. Sometimes the stairs were very steep and uneven. Since we were tired, our legs were shaky, increasing the risk of tripping. Yossep and Saul were extremely helpful, especially on the steepest downhill stairs. Becky and I tried our best not to feel like little old ladies in need of a young man to help us down the stairs, but…sometimes it was really necessary. There are a couple tunnels on the trail which aren't long, but they are dark. And have stairs INSIDE the tunnel. It was impossible to see how steep the stairs were or where to put our feet. Saul absolutely insisted we wait for him to help us through there and I did not argue. Becky tried to argue, but I sided strongly with Saul. We had survived 2.5 days of hiking at that point and we were one day away from Machu Picchu. The last thing we needed at that point was a twisted ankle or to fall and get a concussion from hitting our heads on the rocks.

We were extremely lucky to have such knowledgeable, kind, helpful guides on the hike with us. The night before the hike began, when Miguel assured me that I would be fine because there would be **three Inca warriors** on the Inca Trail, I decided at that point to do my very best to place all of my trust in the guides. If I was going to make it out alive, I needed to trust them and do everything they told me to do, without question. That decision did not fail me. These guides knew what they were doing, they were experienced, and they took very good care of us. For a girl as fiercely independent as I am, it was surprisingly east to put my full and complete trust in the three Inca Trail guides, because of the gravity of the situation.

This is an important lesson for me to take from the trail. Sometimes there is no one in my life who has been in a specific situation before and I need to explore uncharted territory on my own. But more often, there are guides around me who have been there, done that, and can give me guidance and advice. I need to trust that these guides have been placed in my life for the purpose of sharing their valuable knowledge and wisdom with me. Just as Miguel, Yossep and Saul were ready and willing to hold my hand and guide me through the treacherous parts of the Inca Trail, who else has been placed in my life to hold my hand through the scary times? What would it feel like for me to let down my guard, give up a portion of my independence, and learn to trust and rely on these guides? Might that also feel life-giving and life-saving, just as it did on the hike?

I thought how, despite my fierce independent nature, there had been times when following the advice of a guide had saved me. After my divorce, I started attending a new church and I met a wise and friendly woman in her 70s named Jayne. Her story was remarkably like mine, so much so that I started calling her my "maxi-me." (You know, the opposite of a mini-me from the Austin Powers movies…but since Jayne is older than me, I called her my "maxi-me.") Jayne had been divorced before, many years earlier, and was someone who had been where I was and knew what it felt like to be a single, divorced mother in the church. After her divorce, Jayne had remarried and had many years of love and happiness. But unfortunately, her husband became ill and died, not long before I met Jayne. So it was providence that I met Jayne when I did, because she not only knew and understood what it was like to be divorced and a single working mother, she also knew what it was like to go through the grief process.

Jayne was one of the first people I sought out after Ron died. We spent time together hiking with her dog, and Jayne would listen to my heartache and offer me some insight into the grief process. I was drowning in a sea of grief. At a time when I was flailing, Jayne came alongside me as a guide. She had been where I was before, she knew what it felt like, and she knew what had worked for her. She gave me advice and guidance, she spent time with me, and she walked with me during a very difficult point in my life. She was able to provide unique guidance and direction, since she had been on the same road I was walking. She was a gift of God to me at that difficult point in my life. She was a guide, an Inca warrior given to me, and I trusted her wisdom implicitly.

Chapter 12: The Mountains are Always Watching You

"On a hike, the days pass with the wind, the sun, the stars; movement is powered by a belly full of food and water, not a noxious tankful of fossil fuels. On a hike, you're less a job title and more a human being. A periodic hike not only stretches the limbs but also reminds us: Wow, there's a big old world out there." –Ken Ilgunas

I must confess, Saul was my favorite guide. Now, Miguel and Yossep were absolutely amazing too. They were great. Miguel was the leader in charge of our entire group, he directed the work of the two assistant guides and the team of some 30+ porters, and he was ultimately in charge of the 15 family members hiking. He quite literally kept me alive. Yossep was funny, kind, and extremely knowledgeable. But Saul is my favorite, if for no other reason than because he walked with Becky and me the most, so we got to know him the best.

Something Saul said to us regularly was "the mountains are always watching." This sounds creepy, but in the moment, at the time, it was really reassuring. When we expressed sadness at leaving Perú, at breaking up the 15-person family that had become so close on the trail, Saul's response was "the mountains are always watching." I'm not entirely sure what he meant by this, but I have a few ideas and regardless of what he meant, I can explain what it means to me.

As we hiked on the Inca Trail, we were always, always surrounded by mountains. Perhaps that is common sense, I mean, we were in the middle of the Andes. But on the trail, with no cars, no buildings, nothing around, there was a very real sense of our insignificance amid the giant mountains surrounding us. Particularly on the second day of the hike, once we were above the tree line, there was nothing obstructing our view of the mountains. The mountains were tall and brown, covered in grasses; some of the peaks in the distance were snowcapped. On the third day of the hike, we were in the cloud forest where the mountains were lush and vivid green jungle. Whichever area, brown or green mountains, they were always surrounding us. There was a very real feeling that the mountains were alive. That sounds eerie or weird, and maybe it was the sleep deprivation and physical exhaustion that we experienced on the hike, but the mountains were so close and omnipresent, it was almost as if they were alive, watching. Hopefully watching over us, keeping us safe. Hopefully approving of our presence in their midst.

Of course, maybe it only felt like this because Saul kept saying that the mountains were always watching, so it became a self-fulfilling prophecy. That is entirely possible.

Also, our super-knowledgeable guides taught us that in the Inca religion, nature is sacred—lakes, trees, rivers, but especially mountains. These formations rise up from the natural world toward the sky and offer a connection. I suspect Saul had this in mind when he told us the mountains were always watching. The sacred, the divine, is with us.

I consider myself to be a fairly spiritual person under normal circumstances. But on the trail, when everything comfortable and easy and familiar was stripped away, I had to lean significantly on my spirituality for the power to keep going. I believe that God placed me on that trail for a purpose and was going to see me through to the end. I believed that very strongly, and yet, it was so difficult that sometimes I had to keep reminding myself of that with each step. I am here for a reason. I am not alone. God placed me here for a purpose; God will not abandon me. Those were some of my mantras that I repeated in my head even on the first day. Even on the "easy day."

"The mountains are always watching" is another way of saying, I believe, that God is with me. The sacred, the divine, the universe, the mountains…whichever word I choose, I believe that they point to the same spiritual lesson. I am not alone; the mountains are always watching. Even when it's hard, the mountains are always watching. Even when I am led to the windowless room in the hospital, the mountains are always watching. Even when it's late and I'm exhausted and I've had a bad day at work and my children have homework and evening activities and they're hungry and the cat threw up on the living room floor again and I have a headache, even then, the mountains are still watching. And they will not let me fail.

Chapter 13: Accept Help

> *"Getting over the stigma of needing to appear as if I do it all myself took about 12 months. I finally realized that the only way to be a successful, happy mother, founder, wife, and daughter was to accept the help that was being offered to me."* - *Julia Hartz*

In chapter 11 we talked about the lesson of listening to and trusting the guides in charge of our group, because they were super experienced and had led people just like me over the mountain before. When they offered an outstretched hand to get me through a difficult part on the trail, my job was to accept that hand without question and be grateful for its existence. So, what's left to talk about here? What else is there to learn about accepting help?

Sometimes there are clear guides in our life: mentors, people who have experienced something before, and who are in our life to lead us through it. But other times, help is offered by a complete stranger, or by a friend who isn't experienced and just cares about us. Sometimes we need to just let our guard down and accept help. We need to recognize that just as we want to help others, others want to help us.

I learned this lesson over and over on the trail. Sometimes the help was in the form of a kind word of encouragement from a fellow hiker as he or she was passing me along the trail. This was especially the case on the second day of the hike, when it was all uphill, and a lot of people passed me. It was equally true of the fourth and final day of the hike, which we haven't discussed yet, but it was when I was at my lowest point. When people passed me, we would often exchange a word or two of encouragement. We got to recognize many of the people from other groups (we were traveling the same trail over four days) and so we would give a little wave and ask how they were doing. Or they would pass by me as I was pulled off to the side trying to slow my breathing, and they would say something positive and supportive to me as they did. It's amazing how much of a help it is to hear a stranger say to me, "You're doing great!"

But there are two reactions I could have to those words from the stranger. On one hand, I could be grumpy and negative and think, "Yeah, I'm doing so awesome that you and everyone else out here are passing me! I'm doing THE WORST on this trail, but thanks for noticing!" That would be one way of reacting. Or, I could answer them back with my mantra, "Thanks! Always moving forward!" And think to myself that no matter how slow I'm going, I'm still moving forward, and be bolstered by their words. This was a lesson in accepting help, even when it doesn't seem like help. When my mind needed a boost of positivity, I could accept that help from my fellow travelers.

Sometimes our help and encouragement came from the unlikeliest of sources. On the third day of hiking, the trail started out with several grueling hours uphill before switching over to hour after hour of descending. On the first few hours of uphill, Becky and I found ourselves once again counting 35 steps and then stopping to breathe. Early on we saw a man about 60-65 years old with two backpacks—one on his back and the other on his front. I jokingly commented to him, "Whoa! You're doing double duty here?" He explained that his sister was not feeling well so he was carrying her bag. I immediately felt a little bad for my joke, and I told him what an amazing brother he was. I wished him good luck at getting to the summit which surely was almost there.[2]

A little while later, we met up with two ladies, also about 60-65. We soon realized we were walking at about the same pace, and we chatted about it. These ladies were doing 30 steps (or paces, as they called it) and then resting, while we were doing 35. We decided to team up and walk together at our 35 paces. They told us they were from northern Canada and one of them wasn't feeling well that morning. She was the sister of the man we had met earlier, so we shared with her how we saw her brother and thought he was so kind and amazing for carrying her bag. She was walking with her sister-in-law (wife of the man with two bags). As it turns out, her brother and

---

[2] It wasn't.

sister-in-law do a lot of hiking and had encouraged her to take on the Inca Trail. She fell ill on the second day— probably altitude sickness—so her brother was carrying her bag and her sister-in-law was walking slowly with her, getting her up the mountain step by step.

My experience with these Canadian women validated every stereotype you've ever heard: Canadians are supremely kind and friendly. They were amazing. In their sickness and exhaustion, they were encouraging us! They also had a fantastic perspective. They were the ones that shared with us their thoughts about how different the view is each 30 (or 35) paces. We would trudge up the stairs for 35 steps, and then turn around to look at the valley. Gorgeous view. Catch our breath, trudge up 35 more stairs, and turn around again. Gorgeous view again, but entirely different this time. The four of us would say out loud what speaks to us—look at those trees, look at that pond, look at those rocks over there. We were each captured by something different. It was a wonderful experience, walking with those women. We forgot about how awful we felt, about how our lungs were gasping for air, about how our legs were sore from the days before.

We were in the moment, enraptured in the glory of this beautiful planet, and in the glory of meeting and enjoying beautiful people who live on this planet.

These women were a help to me, more than I can really explain or understand. Had I been closed up in my own mind, trudging up the stairs and locking out thoughts of anything else, I would have missed it. I would have missed the beauty of their perspective, of their impact on my life. We crossed paths with those ladies several more times on the trail, and each time it was a gift of positivity and joy. Interacting with them helped me by shifting my perspective and lifting me out of my misery for a short time. It showed me that I wasn't alone. I mean, I knew that because I was walking with Becky, but it showed us that we were not alone. We were in excellent company and it reminded us that taking it slow isn't necessarily a bad thing. It allowed us the time to fully savor the beauty of the Andes. Even though our lungs needed extra time to function, our eyes were still working. We could use that time wisely looking around in amazement and awe at the beauty that surrounded us. Thanks, Canadian friends, for helping us through a difficult part of the trail.

I have talked a lot about Becky—since we did a lot of the hiking together—and my sister Kellie, since she is my sister and my rock. But I've barely mentioned Cindy, who was absolutely one of the biggest helps to me on this trip. Over and over and over again, I needed to accept her help without letting my mind go into a place of guilt. In reality, I couldn't have done this trip without her. I met Cindy back in 2004 when we started working together. She had been in the job longer than me and offered a lot of on-the-job training—the kind of information that the supervisor doesn't provide, but an experienced peer does. Years later, when Cindy moved on to another job, we continued to get together, mostly to run races. Last year we ran two Ragnar relay races together. If you don't know what those are, then you should definitely Google it and sign up for the nearest race to you. They are a ton of fun. And exhausting, but mostly fun. It's also a way to really get to know a group of people by living and eating and running with them for two days.

Cindy was also very close with Ron, and his death affected her just as it affected me. I will be forever indebted to Cindy for the way she cared for me after Ron passed. He died on a Friday afternoon; his funeral was eight days later on a Saturday morning. That Saturday happened to be my 37th birthday. As an adult, birthdays aren't really much fun anyway, but I had been planning to spend that day together with my children at the beach. Instead, I was delivering a eulogy in front of a packed church. After the funeral was over and my mom and Kellie and her family left, I found myself alone in my house with my children. I remember lying facedown on my dining room floor, unable to move. My eight-year-old daughter saw my pain and didn't know what to do to help, so she stretched herself out on top of me, trying to pull the pain out of my body and into hers. At that moment of utmost despair, I got a text from Cindy that simply said, "Are you ok?" I wrote back and said, "No." She said, "Are you alone?" I said, "My kids are here." She wrote back the most beautiful text ever: "I will be there in 10 minutes." Cindy's presence that night gave me the ability to feed my children dinner, to exist with them, and to get them to bed. I don't know what I would have done that night without her, but she gave me the strength and the power to be a mom. I couldn't do it alone, but with her there with me, I could find the courage to do it.

Accept help when it's offered. It's okay.

On the Inca Trail, Cindy was my tent-mate. Things get pretty close when you're sharing a tent. On the first day, we hiked together and figured things out as we went. She had a bag with her that wasn't cooperating so we strategized ways to adjust it until it worked for her. She and I teamed up for the bathroom, one of us (often her) carrying the toilet paper as we made our way to wherever the bathroom was. At the end of the second day, after I had hiked the hardest hike of my life and finally made it to the camp, overwhelmed and bawling, Cindy and Kellie were there to greet me, to unlace my boots, to help me soak my feet in water, and to keep me going. That night, when it was the coldest, Cindy shared her extra blanket, which kept me warm enough to actually get some sleep. Cindy and I laughed together and cried together in our tent. We debriefed from our day, shared what we thought were our hardest parts and what we found most beautiful. On the fourth day when we walked to the bathrooms and

I discovered I was ill (spoiler alert) Cindy went back to the tent and brought me back some Imodium. Cindy was an amazing help to me, and I don't believe I could have completed the trail without her. Kellie told me later that she and Becky were talking about all of the things they liked about Cindy, and at the top of the list was the way she took care of me.

So. I'm an independent person by nature. I hate having to rely on other people. I want to be Supermom and take care of my kids by myself while handling my job and all of my other responsibilities. Sometimes this seems to work okay, and I get complacent, thinking that I really can do it all on my own. And then something happens. My world gets rocked, the rug gets pulled out from under me, and I am suddenly unable to do it all. I need to learn to accept the help that is given me. Whether that help is in the form of a kind word of encouragement from a passing stranger, or from a fellow traveler's refreshing perspective, or if that help is in the form of a good friend who journeys side by side with me. The Inca Trail taught me that it is folly to think we can do anything alone. We are creatures designed to live in community.

Just as I desire to help others, I must accept that help myself. I am so grateful for the helpers that have come alongside of me in the difficult parts of my journey. I hope I can repay their help in some small way by coming alongside others as they walk through difficult waters.

Chapter 14: Pull Over for the Porters

"As you start to walk out on the way, the way appears." -Rumi

As I mentioned way back in chapter 1, there are only 500 people allowed on the Inca Trail each day. Of that number, about 200 are tourist hikers, and the other 300 are guides and porters. When we were there, some tour providers had people who carried their own belongings in large packs, but for the most part, the porters were there to carry the personal belongs, tents, food and cooking supplies for everyone. The hike simply wouldn't have been possible without them. Not at that elevation, not for that length of time.

The porters for each tour company would wear a uniform. G Adventures' color is purple, so our porters wore purple t-shirts and pants. There were two G Adventures groups on the trail, ours and a smaller group led by a guide named Victor. So when we saw the purple porters, we didn't know if they were our group's or Victor's porters. No matter: they were porters, they wore the G Adventure color, they were part of us.

I will confess, the concept of porters was a little unsettling at times. These were paid employees, but it felt a little bit like we were condoning slave labor. These individuals had HUMONGOUS packs to carry. Someone carried the propane tank for the camp stove, someone else carried the stove itself. Those had to be heavy. They carried all of our duffel bags—several duffels per each porter—they carried the table we sat at for meals, the stools we sat on, and every other thing imaginable. When we were deciding which tour company to use, we read (and our travel agent told us) that G Adventures was a reputable company that paid their porters good wages and treated them well. But still, these men did seriously difficult physical labor for days, and they slept in very tight quarters at night. Most of the porters were indigenous Incas who spoke Quechua and were members of the lowest social class in Peruvian society.

Miguel told us that he had been a porter for years, before becoming a guide with G Adventures. He said that this was a good job for these men, and they were able to provide for their families with the money they earn. That made me feel a little better, but it was still outside my comfort zone. The porters were very, very impressive. They would often run along the trail, especially the flat and downhill portions. I saw them stop and rest *occasionally* while going uphill, but not often enough. Particularly not when considering the HUGE weights they were carrying.

When we started out on the first day, we were given some advice from the guides. We were told that if porters were coming up the trail, we should stop and hug the mountain and let them pass on the outside. As we were hiking, it became a cry that would go out among the trail. Someone would yell, "Porters! Porters coming!" and we would know to get over, and then we would shout ahead to the people in front of us, who would follow suit. We would hear the "porter!" warning echoing up and back across the trail. This would happen multiple times a day as each of the groups followed the same practice. We would wake up early, have breakfast and be hiking by 6:30 AM (except for the last day, when we started at 4:30 AM.) The porters would tear down the camp and set out, passing the groups along the way. Then they would rush to set up lunch. The same process would happen after lunch, when the porters would tear everything down and then pass us along the trail on their way to set up camp for the night and start dinner. So twice a day, 300 porters would pass by on the trail.

It became a comforting dance: shouting "Porter!" and then pulling over to the left so that the porters could pass around us. I'm not sure why it was comforting, the familiarity of it perhaps. It was a sign somehow that we were actually making progress. We were moving forward, learning the ropes; things weren't so completely strange anymore. We were getting the hang of this, and we were seasoned hikers now. It was the same feeling of satisfaction I got from seeing dirt accumulate on my boots. I would excitedly show Cindy, saying, "Look! Look at this dirt! These hiking boots have *been places!*" Miguel taught us how to say thank you in the Quechua language. When possible, I would to remember to say thanks to the porters as they passed, whether they were G Adventures porters or not. These men worked so hard, and their work made it possible for me to hike the trail, so I was indebted to them.

Earlier we discussed the lesson of going at our own pace, and how that applies to life outside the Inca Trail. Pulling over for the porters is a similar lesson. This is about us giving grace to others, to allow *them* to go at *their* own pace on their journey, even when (perhaps especially when) their pace is much faster than ours. Maybe what they need from us is to just get out of the way and give them the space they need, and wish them well on their journey. Pulling over for the porters also reminds us to yield to others who are carrying heavy burdens...maybe burdens that aren't outwardly visible. Maybe they just look like someone in a hurry, or too rushed to care about us, but under the surface, they are bearing a heavy load. There may not be anything we can do to assist those with their heavy burdens; we can't remove them or help carry them. But we can step aside and give them the space they need, and possibly utter a word of encouragement or gratitude to them as they pass by.

A few years ago, I experienced the end of a very close friendship. We had been friends for 15+ years, and I thought we would be friends forever. For reasons I don't understand and likely won't ever understand, that friendship ended. That hurt, horribly. The friendship ended about eight months after Ron died, so it was a time in my life when I was reeling. Rudderless. Desperately trying to keep my head above the waters of grief, but unsure how to do that. The loss of this friendship was a brutal blow at a time when everything was already hard. I still don't fully understand it, and it still hurts. This isn't the part of this book where I say that hiking the Inca Trail for four days helped me fully and completely understand why this friendship had to end and gave me a great peace about it. I wish this were that type of book, but it's not. Rather, it occurs to me that I need to apply the "pull over for the porters" lesson here, to this friendship. I don't know what burdens she is carrying. I thought we were close enough friends that we shared our burdens with one another, but we are human and we often withhold pain and difficulty and don't even show it to our close friends. Or maybe it's not that altruistic of a burden—perhaps she had just long ago grown tired of me and didn't know how to tell me. Whatever the reason, she had a heavy burden to bear and she was moving quickly through her life journey—much more quickly than I was able to travel at that point. I remain hurt by the way that she passed me by, moved on quickly, didn't even look back to see if I was upright and journeying again. But perhaps it's time that I step aside and give her the grace to travel at her own pace. I should utter a word of gratitude to her for the role she has had in my life, and then I need to take up my slower, methodical tempo once she has passed by. Maybe I will get to a point in life, as I did on the Inca Trail, when this exercise becomes comfortable and comforting to me...this dance we do of going our own pace and allowing others the space to go at their own pace, even when it means they journey on, out of our lives.

Chapter 15: The Journey is Yours Alone; No One Else Can Live It.

"To travel is to take a journey into yourself." - *Danny Kaye*

In my last book, I talked about a girls weekend beach tradition that my girlfriends and I used to have. On those trips, we had a motto: "Define your own beach fun," which essentially meant we should each feel free to do what we want that weekend, and not feel guilty. If we want to get in the water, great! Do it! If we don't like water and just want to sit on the sand and read all day, great! Do that! For this one weekend a year, we can be absolutely selfish and define our own beach fun and not feel bad about it.

This phrase did not apply on the Inca Trail. For starters, I would hardly call the experience "fun" in the usual sense. It was deeply satisfying to accomplish the hike. Walking through the Andes, getting to experience that beautiful scenery all around, to feel completely immersed in the wonders of this planet was awe-inspiring. Being there as part of a family, with our three Inca warriors, it was deeply satisfying and soul-filling. But...not really fun.

The Inca Trail did teach me, however, that the journey is unique for each person hiking. We all brought our own baggage with us, our own "stuff". We were there for different reasons. Some of us in the group, mainly the younger "kids" (and I'm allowed to call people in their early 20s kids, since I am now entering my fifth decade of life), were there as part of an extended trip across South America. The Inca Trail hike was sandwiched between other excursions and visits to a number of different countries. Others were travelling for their own reasons. Kellie and I were there ostensibly to celebrate my 40th birthday. But in reality, I believe we were put there at that point in time and with that group of people, for a purpose that only God knows. The four of us travelling together—Becky, Kellie, Cindy and I—each have a journey that is uniquely ours, and the Inca Trail fits into our greater journeys in some way that is unique to each of us.

Much like my girlfriends and I used to "define our own beach fun," we got to define our own Inca Trail journey. We got to physically hike it at whatever pace and with whatever rhythm we needed. Our ensuing emotional experience got to be as deep and cathartic as each needed. Just because I came away from the Inca Trail deeply moved and profoundly changed as a person doesn't mean that anyone else would have the same experience. I believe all of the elements are there for such an experience, but it is up to each of us to define the journey as we see fit. No one else can experience it for us.

In life, we are each on a journey. From birth to death and a million places in between, we are all journeying through this world. Our journeys are uniquely ours. And when we hit rough patches, when the trail is hard, steep, and treacherous, there is no one else to live our journey for us. We can ask a guide to come alongside us and hold our hand through such times, but that guide cannot transport us across without us doing the work. No one can live our life for us. Whatever path is set before us, whatever the universe has in store for each of us, it is up to us alone to experience it and live it out. Even when it gets dark and difficult.

Chapter 16: The Inca Trail Will Break You and Remake You if You Let It.

"The trail is the thing, not the end of the trail. Travel too fast and you miss all you are traveling for." -Louis L'Amour

I've described the first and second days of the hike well—first day flat (mostly) but still really hard; second day uphill forever and ever and insanely hard, then a few hours of downhill that was different, but still pretty hard. Then to camp where we spent the coldest night of the trip. That night was so cold that they warned us when we got up at night to go to the bathroom, we had to go slow and acclimate ourselves to the cold air. We needed to get out of our sleeping bags and stay in our tent for a few minutes before unzipping into the night air, for fear of jarring our systems too quickly and getting sick. Part of the altitude sickness, I guess. Anyway, against all odds, I slept remarkably well that night. I woke up still feeling nauseous but thanks to the miracle anti-nausea medication from my fellow travelers, I was good to go.

We were told the third day was the longest, but would be mostly downhill. It was true. The first few hours were uphill toward the second highest elevation, but after that it was all downhill. Sometimes a gentle sloping decline, but often it was more severe with stairs upon stairs upon stairs. It was exhausting, difficult work. I used my poles as much as possible, but my knees and calves were terribly sore. I never thought about how difficult it is on the muscles to go downstairs until I had to go down thousands of huge rock stairs and my muscles made it abundantly clear to me just how difficult it was. It got so painful that all I wanted to do was stop. And yet starting back again after stopping was agony. I was so ready to be at the end of the trail.

While I was dealing with all of the difficult physical aspects to the trail on the third day, my emotions were also going crazy. I had done so well on the first and second days to keep them bottled up, but surviving the second day and seeing Miguel waiting for me, and hearing his words to me...it was too much for me. I spent day three raw and with my emotions very close to the surface. The first part of the day was when we met the two ladies from Canada who were doing a 30 pace rhythm, since one of them wasn't feeling well. Those ladies touched me in a very deep way—the way they cared for each other was beautiful and despite feeling ill, they had the most amazingly positive outlook. Their perspective was wonderful and it touched me deeply.

Once we surpassed the summit of that mountain, we began descending into the cloud forest. It was so wonderfully beautiful and entirely different than what we had seen prior to that point. The trees were lush and green with vines hanging down; there were orchids and beautiful bright flowers and hummingbirds everywhere. It was too gorgeous for words and the beauty of my surroundings, plus my already raw emotions, brought me to tears. Or maybe the tears were from my sore legs. Possibly both.

And yet, despite the agony and the emotion of it all, there was a growing sense of positivity. I had survived the hard second day of the hike and had gotten past Dead Woman's Pass. I had made it through the coldest night at camp (and had slept pretty well!) and I had made it up and over the second highest peak. While the hike was long and hard on my body going down all those steps, I knew I could do it. I was doing it. Every step I took, though it hurt, was proof to me that I was doing this well. No longer did I doubt that I could make it all the way to Machu Picchu; I knew I was succeeding. I felt lighter and freer, as I was shedding some of my emotional baggage along the way. I felt like I was on my way toward the spiritual enlightenment that I was hoping to find at the end of this trail. Maybe (spoiler alert) I was just getting a little cocky.

Nevertheless, the experience taught me that the Inca Trail would break me and remake me if I allowed it. If I submitted myself to the process (and I did) then the trail would do its magic. I was systematically broken down over days one and two of the trail—I was brought to my limit physically, emotionally and spiritually. I got to the point where I felt hopeless. But then the trail had me right where I was meant to be, and I could begin the process of being reborn. I had to learn to accept help. I learned the limits of my capabilities, but I also learned that when I accept help from others, my capabilities increase and become limitless.

I think this is sort of the big lesson that life is trying to teach us. Life isn't easy, we know that. Sometimes, those really big, really hard things are going to break us down. They will humble us until we get to the point where we feel we have nothing. But how we respond to that is up to us—do we allow that process to work in us? Do we surrender ourselves to God or to the universe or to the process and trust that we will be remade into something new? Or do we dig our heels in and shake our fist yelling, "It's not fair!" I have had times when life has tried to change me and I have dug in my heels, willing things to stay the same while I desperately try to hold on to something that isn't there anymore. That doesn't ever work out. And so I've been learning—through Ron's death, through the Inca Trail, and through several other experiences in between—that I need to surrender and trust. The Inca Trail broke me a little bit, but I surrendered myself to that process, and on day three I began to see glimmers of hope that I would be remade into something new. Life is beautiful like that.

Chapter 17: Nothing is Impossible on the Inca Trail

"You need to aim beyond what you are capable of. You must develop a complete disregard for where your abilities end. Try to do things that you're incapable of...if you think you're incapable of running a company, make that your aim. Make your vision of where you want to be a reality. Nothing is impossible." -Paul Arden

When we stopped for lunch on day three, I was not feeling great again. I was taking the anti-nausea pills every six hours, but they weren't working as well anymore. I had no appetite, and the nausea was starting to overtake me. It was frustrating because by lunch on the third day, everything difficult was behind me. Well, for the most part. All of the major uphill parts were done, and we were descending into the cloud forest. The trail

126

was beautiful and not difficult on the lungs anymore. My legs were screaming in pain and we kept going down more and more stairs, so that was difficult. But compared to the day before, it was doable. Following this stop for lunch, we had just the afternoon of hiking, then we would be at camp for the night. The next day, we had only about three miles of hiking before we got to Machu Picchu. We were so close!

Miguel told us the chefs had something special in store for us that day at lunch. Many people were sick—either altitude sickness or an intestinal virus or both, it was unknown. And then there was me; I didn't think I was sick with either of those things, I was just exhausted and queasy. But we tried to work up some excitement for this surprise from the chefs. It turned out they had cooked enough food for an army and were serving us a buffet lunch. Except there wasn't really room for a buffet line in the tight quarters of the dining tent, so we had to pass the food from one to another, over and over around the table. The food was gorgeous—radish roses in the salad and other fancy touches to make the dishes worthy of the Food Network. However, given that many of us were sick at that point, I was not super excited about eating food that had been passed from sick person to sick person before it got to me. That didn't really matter though, because I could barely eat anyway. I wanted to. The food looked delicious, but I was struggling with terrible nausea.

After lunch Miguel got excited again and said the chefs had one more surprise for us. Unbelievably, they brought out a beautiful cake, fully frosted and decorated, that said "Welcome to the Inca Trail." These chefs were magicians. Miguel explained that they had gotten up at 4:00 AM that morning to bake a cake in a pot, somehow, over the propane camp stove. Then they hiked for a few hours over the second highest elevation on the trail, carrying the cake. And when they got to the lunch spot, they frosted and decorated the cake. Oh yeah, while also preparing enough food for a small army. And I'm sure the cake was delicious, but I wouldn't know. I ended up giving my slice of cake to Cindy. It was frustrating that I was again feeling so ill. It was frustrating that I couldn't be like the rest of the team, enjoying the buffet lunch and celebration cake.

All too soon we heard Miguel shout, "Backpacks on!" and it was time to head back out to the trail. I was tired, weak, and ready for the hiking to be over. It was so close to the end I could almost taste it, but I had to keep in the zone. I couldn't think about how much I wanted to be done or how close we were, or anything other than putting one foot in front of the other, carefully, and not falling as we continued to descend many stone steps. The afternoon pressed on. Becky and I were moving as fast as we could, but it never seemed to be fast enough. Saul was with us again, helping us through the stretches that were dangerous. We passed by several more Inca ruins, and Saul encouraged us to take as long as we wanted to enjoy them and take pictures, but I felt an enormous pressure to keep going. When we left camp that morning at 6:30 AM, we were told to pack our headlamps in our daypacks in case we didn't get to camp that night until after dark. I knew that was a possibility, but I wanted to avoid it if at all possible. And so we kept moving forward, always putting our poles on the next step.

At one point Saul gave us a choice. He said there would be a fork in the road with one way leading to a spectacular set of Inca terraces that we could explore and get a fabulous view of the Urubamba river valley. However, that way would add 1-2 hours to the trip. The other way would be shorter. I hated that we were given this choice. I didn't want to miss out on anything, just because I was moving slowly. I wanted to get to the end and be able to say that I had done it all, every single step, no shortcuts. And yet...I couldn't justify going the long route. At some point I had to listen to my body a tiny bit, and I knew I wouldn't have time to go the long route. It was getting dark and after three days of endless torture, my body was shutting down. I would have to make do with seeing pictures from Kellie and Cindy who would undoubtedly take the long way around.

When we got to the fork in the road, it was 5:00 PM and dusk was settling in. We arrived at the fork around the same time as another traveler we had seen several times on the trail. He told us his guide had given him 5:00 as the cutoff point—if he arrived at the fork earlier than that, he could go the long way. Otherwise, he needed to turn right at the fork and head directly to camp. This was added proof to me that we were doing the right thing. Unfortunately, the trail changed when we forked off to the right. Gone were all the cobblestone rocks, and in place was a sandy dirt trail, which was quite slippery. Every muscle in my legs was screaming at me to stop this madness, and here I was giving them a new obstacle. Becky fell not too long after starting on this point in the trail. Saul came running and helped her get settled back into hiking, but she definitely kept a slower pace at that point. I was determined to finish. I just needed to be done as soon as possible, because I was feeling so ill. So I broke off from Becky and Saul and kept at my own pace. My only thoughts were on getting to camp and finishing this day. It took more than an hour from the fork; I didn't make it back to camp until after 6:00 PM. It was mostly dark so I was glad to have my headlamp with me for the last bit of the hike. I got to the tent and immediately collapsed. I was so thoroughly exhausted. I had done the three hardest hiking days, but at that point I had no celebration in me. Only agony and exhaustion.

Collapsing in a heap inside my tent was the only option, but I felt little relief at sitting down. I knew I was so close to the end and I would see Machu Picchu the next day but at that moment it didn't mean much. If someone offered me a shower and a hotel room bed at that point instead of sleeping in a tent one more night and hiking the last three miles to see Machu Picchu...I wonder if I would have taken that deal.

To make matters worse, Kellie came to the tent and started giving me the report of our team. Several more people had succumbed to vomiting and diarrhea. I was already feeling nauseous and shaky but as soon as Kellie said this, my brain told me it was inevitable. I would be next. The idea was implanted in my brain and I couldn't take it out.

Our camp that night was not wonderful. We were camping in a common area with all the other groups nearby. We had a small section just for us, but we could hear the other groups all around us. We had to hike pretty far (up and down more sandy dirt trail steps!!) to get to the bathroom, and it was the worst bathroom yet, made all the more terrible because so many groups were using it. Our camp was pretty far from it which I hated because it was so far to get to and my legs hurt so much, and yet the stench was so bad, I wouldn't want to be anywhere within a 300 foot radius anyway. It was a real conundrum. Also, we had descended so much that day that the climate was different. The air was hot and humid and the inside of our tent was stuffy and warm.

Saul and Becky arrived at camp not long after I did and very quickly we were assembled for our last dinner together. We were a bedraggled group that night. The porters had made a small supper, since lunch was so big. That was smart because few of us had any appetite. One young 21-year-old boy from New Zealand named Toby had to keep excusing himself from the dinner table to go vomit. He impressed me so much by how upbeat he was, despite his circumstances. Here he is a young 21-year-old kid (practically a kid) all alone in a foreign country, hiking and camping and doing the near-impossible and now he is sick as a dog. And yet he was not only staying positive, he was also super polite. As he got up from the dinner table to go throw up, he would politely say, "Excuse me for a moment, please." Incredible. And there I was, not vomiting. What excuse did I have for my negativity?

Many times on the trail, when it was difficult and I was starting to think it might not be possible for me to finish, Saul or Miguel or Yossep would say to me, "Nothing is impossible on the Inca Trail." Miguel said to me in Ollantaytambo, the night before we left. I wanted to believe him then, but I didn't yet. After three long days on the trail, though, and hearing countless times from our Inca Warriors that nothing is impossible on the Inca Trail, my doubts were fading. Seeing Toby stay positive and polite and upbeat that night at dinner, despite his horrible circumstances, I was starting to see the truth in that. Nothing is impossible on the Inca Trail.

It is tradition on the Inca Trail that the family members each pool their tips together for the porters and present the gift to them on the third night after dinner. Miguel told us before we left that he would ask someone to make a speech when presenting the gift to them, and he typically asks the best Spanish speaker to make the speech. My Spanish is certainly rusty, but since I ostensibly have a Bachelor's degree in the language, I wasn't surprised when Miguel asked me to make the speech. In fact, I had been kind of writing it in my head while on the trail. It's one thing, however, to give a speech in Spanish in your head. It's quite another to give a speech in Spanish out loud in front of 14 teammates, 37 porters and three guides. Oh yeah, and I was mentally and physically and emotionally exhausted to the point of my body involuntarily shutting down. But I gave it my best effort.

I did my best to convey to the porters, on behalf of our entire family, that they were amazing. They were machines. There I was, struggling to get up the mountain with my puny little daypack. I was huffing and puffing and stopping to breathe. Meanwhile, the porters were carrying these HUGE GIANT HUMONGOUS packs on their backs, and they were RUNNING up and down the mountains. I attempted to convey to them how awestruck we were by their dedication and abilities. Nothing is impossible on the Inca Trail…but only because we had this team of amazing porters there to assist us. Without the porters, I would have had to carry all of my gear, including my sleeping bag and tent, and set up camp every night after hiking. That would have been impossible. The same is true for our two wonderful chefs. Unfortunately

I was too nauseous to really appreciate the food, but they worked so hard to give us amazing five-star-restaurant quality foods. Nothing is impossible on the Inca Trail…but if we had to carry and cook our own food every night…that would have been impossible. Instead, we had the assistance of porters and chefs who took care of us and enabled us to do the impossible. That's the message I tried to convey.

Most importantly, we had three Inca Warriors on our trip with us. Nothing is impossible on the Inca Trail, but without them, it would have been. My speech was directed to the porters, but I couldn't resist tacking on something at the end to thank our guides. I told them that one of the reasons I went on this trip was to prove to myself that even at my age, even as I was approaching 40, I could still do difficult things in life. I could still do anything I put my mind to, even though it be hard, and exhausting, and long. But what I learned while hiking, is that yes, I can do anything I put my mind to, but not alone. I must accept help from my team. On this trip, my team consisted of 14 family members, 37 porters, two chefs, and three Inca Warriors. And with the help of my team, indeed, nothing was impossible on the Inca Trail.

This lesson is true outside of the Inca Trail, and I have been learning it for quite some time. When I got divorced, I assembled a team of friends around me that I called "Team Kim" and I will forever be grateful to Team Kim. They helped me look at houses to buy, helped me buy furniture, buy a piano from Craigslist and get it moved to my new house; they helped me pack up and move, and then they helped me paint my daughter's bedroom and several other rooms in the new place. They drove my moving van, assembled furniture, handled inquiries from friends and neighbors who didn't know about the divorce, and generally held me up at a time when I couldn't find my footing and didn't know how to stand. Similarly, when Ron died and the rug was pulled out from under me, I survived only by the help of my teammates. From Kellie and my mom who dropped everything and drove eight hours to come and get me at the beach, to Cindy who came the night of his funeral to help me be a parent to my children, to countless others whose love and care held me up and kept me going at a time when I didn't know how to go forward.

Nothing is impossible in this life. We may not all be able to stay positive and polite like Toby in the midst of our trials, but we can keep going…with the help of our teammates. Once we learn to accept the help that is given to us, the possibilities are endless. This is the lesson that the Inca Trail has (once again) taught me.

Chapter 18: The Clouds Will Clear

Then up the ladder of the earth I have risen
Through the awful tangles of lost forests
Up to you, my friend, Macchu Picchu

Pablo Neruda, "The Heights of Macchu Picchu"

After my speech to the porters that night, we presented our tips to them, and then they all made a circle and one by one shook the hands of all 15 family members. It was pretty cool. Miguel pulled me aside and told me he *almost* shed a tear during my speech. I thanked him again for keeping me alive on the trail, and for changing my life. With that, I went to bed and tried to sleep in the stuffy hot tent. It did not go well.

Our wake up time on day four was 3:30 AM. The plan was to start hiking by 4:00 AM a short distance to the security checkpoint. All the groups got in line and waited for the security guard to arrive by 5:00 AM to let the groups through to the Machu Picchu citadel. So when I went to bed that night after dinner, I knew I only had about five hours of potential sleep. I was hoping I could just magically fall right to sleep, like I had the previous night. Instead, the longer I laid in bed in the stuffy hot tent, the sicker I started to feel. I couldn't get comfortable, I was too hot, and my stomach was churning. I found some antacid in my first aid kit (the first time using it!) which helped settle my stomach a bit, but it was becoming increasingly clear that I needed to use the bathroom. I did not want to hike all the way there in the middle of the night, so I laid in bed hoping the feeling would pass. It didn't. I'm not sure I slept at all that night. By 3:30 AM, I was ready to get this day started. Cindy woke up and agreed to make the trek to the bathroom with me.

It was no small feat getting to the bathroom, by the way, since my legs were in deep protest. From three days of intense hiking, and all of the downhill sections of day three, they were more sore than they had ever been. After lying in bed for a few hours, my legs were so stiff they did not want to move. Getting out of the tent at all was nearly impossible and I looked ridiculous trying. Finally I got my legs working enough to make it to the bathroom, with Cindy's help. It was just as disgusting and smelly as it had been the night before. Between already feeling queasy and being near the stench of the toilets, I was gagging. Sadly, once I got inside, I discovered that I had been afflicted with horrible, virulent diarrhea. I will spare the details here, but it was awful. And the "bathroom" as it were, was essentially just a hole in the ground with a sort-of flushing mechanism. So, it was difficult. And miserable.

I came out of the bathroom, and saw Cindy and I just started crying. I said, "Cindy, I'm sick! I can't leave the bathroom yet." She said she would go get me some Imodium, and off she left. 99% of my brain was busy feeling miserable and disgusting, but the remaining 1% was overcome with gratitude for her. I used the bathroom three or more times, each time worse than the last. It was awful and I felt too weak to move. It was as if my body were saying finally, "Enough! You have tormented us for three days straight now. We are done, and you aren't going any further." I stepped out of the bathroom and sat down on a tree root a few steps away from the bathroom, knowing I would need to be inside again shortly. I put my head down and cried as around me other groups were coming and going from the bathroom, excited to be up and ready to see Machu Picchu.

Cindy came and gave me the Imodium and asked me if I would be okay to hike. I said I didn't think I could move, I needed to stay by the bathroom. She must have gone to get Miguel and report my sickness because the next thing I knew, Miguel was next to me, asking me what was happening. I said to him, "I'm sick!" and I cried on his shoulder. Again. All thoughts of Toby and his amazing, mature handling of sickness was gone. I was in full-on crybaby mode. Miguel hugged me and said "Just two more hours, baby, just two more hours." I told him I was sick and needed to stay by the bathroom. He just kept saying, "Just two more hours. Okay? You can do that. Two more hours and then you get to a nice, clean bathroom with a real toilet! You can do this. Just two more hours."

What choice did I have? None. So, I swallowed the Imodium and went and got my daypack and walking poles and started hiking. As it turned out, the line formed not far away and we passed another camp bathroom (also with a horrible stench.) So while our group was waiting, I got one final chance to use the toilet. Then we were off.

Once we got through the checkpoint, we were supposed to have one hour of hiking to the Sun Gate, where we could see the sun rising above Machu Picchu, and then one hour hiking from there down to Machu Picchu. Our whole group was to assemble at the Sun Gate for a group picture with Machu Picchu in the background. Miguel had made it abundantly clear the night before that he was going to have 15 family members at the sun gate in the picture. So, there was not going to be any chance of the group going ahead this time, they would be waiting for Becky and me to show up and all be together. Given my situation that morning, I was feeling the pressure. Saul was stationed at the back of the pack with Becky and me again, and he was doing his best to cheer me up with silly jokes. It wasn't working. He told me to take my time and go at my own pace. I told him I had so little energy and I didn't want to hold everyone up. He told me not to worry about it.

Even in my misery, I was able to grasp a bit of the beauty around me. To start hiking in the dark and watch as the light entered little by little was magical. We had the mountainside to our left and the valley to our right, we could see the clouds and mist hovering in the valley, and it was stunning. Unfortunately, it took nearly all of my faculties to keep my feet moving forward and to will myself not to be sick on the side of the trail, so I didn't get to fully appreciate everything. I took a few pictures (not that they do justice) and kept trying to move forward. I don't know exactly how long we were hiking, but it was well over an hour. The trail seemed endless.

We had been hearing for several days about a set of stairs along the trail, just before the Sun Gate, that were called the "monkey stairs." Alternatively, they were called the "gringo killer" which is not a name I liked. This set of stairs was supposed to be so steep, hikers had to use their hands like a monkey climbing a ladder. I wasn't really looking forward to that, particularly feeling as I was that morning. But I also wanted to be done hiking, so I kept hoping to see the monkey stairs every time I turned a corner. I kept asking Saul, every time I got to some stone stairs on the trail, "Are *these* the monkey stairs?" He kept saying no, which was frustrating. I had so little energy and it was taking everything in me to keep going. I stopped talking to Saul and Becky and kept my mind focused on moving my feet and not getting sick. The Inca Trail is a sacred space, and the thought of getting sick in the midst of such a hallowed, beautiful place...it would have killed me.

This portion of the hike was taking MUCH longer than it was supposed to. My pace was excruciatingly slow, much slower than Becky and I had been going the previous days. I felt terrible about holding our group up at the Sun Gate. I told Saul that they shouldn't wait for me; they should just go on. At first he told me that they would all wait, but after a bit he said he had radioed to Miguel and told them to keep moving. I knew Miguel wanted us all together at the Sun Gate, but I was relieved. I couldn't be the one to hold up the entire group. That would be too much pressure.

Finally, after two or more hours of agonizing hiking, we turned the corner and Saul smiled impishly and said, "These are the monkey stairs." I looked up at them and thought, "this is impossible. I can't do that." But I stopped myself and didn't fully allow that thought to form because I had no choice. Impossible or not, I was going to do it, and on the other side would be Machu Picchu. Saul took my poles for me and showed me how to grab onto the ledges above me with my hands. He cautioned me to find good footing before taking a step, and I was off. After the first couple steps, there was no going back. I couldn't look up because it was too far to go. I couldn't look down because I don't like heights and it would scare me to see how far off the ground I was. I just had to keep going, one foot in front of the other, with my hands always grabbing onto the next step. I couldn't allow any thoughts about how tired I was, or how sore my legs were, or how sick I felt. The only thing I could think about was climbing this stone ladder in the middle of the Peruvian jungle and not falling to my death.

When I got to the top of the monkey stairs, I saw that there was just a little bit further—maybe 200 feet—and we were at the Sun Gate. THE SUN GATE! We had made it! I couldn't believe it. I didn't really believe it. I needed Saul to tell me I wasn't dreaming. Once Becky and Saul got to the top of the monkey stairs, we moved forward for our last little bit. Just before we got there, around the corner came Miguel. I was shocked, since I expected he was gone from the Sun Gate by then. As it turned out, however, the entire group was there, waiting for us. I turned to Saul and told him through tears that he was a liar. (This was an ongoing joke between us and Saul, because he did lie to us sometimes when we needed it. He lied by saying our camp was "just a little farther" and he lied when he said the trail would be "mostly flat." Here, he lied by saying the group had gone on ahead, so I didn't feel bad about going so slowly.) Saul just smiled mischievously and admitted that yes, he had lied. But it was a good lie.

Miguel helped me finish the last few steps of the trail and then gave me a huge hug. Once again, I cried and clung to Miguel and he told me how proud he was of me for getting through it. More tears shed along the Inca Trail! Once I calmed down and dried my tears, I looked through the Sun Gate for my first glimpse of Machu Picchu. The fabled city that had for so long existed only in photographs, this goal that I had been working toward for so long and I saw…clouds. Unbelievable! Kellie came up and told me not to worry about just getting there because I hadn't missed a thing. We couldn't have taken the group picture anyway because the clouds hadn't cleared yet. I looked around and noticed other groups were there too, waiting for the clouds to pass and it felt great that I hadn't missed out on anything because I was slow. I hadn't held the group up; there were still other groups there too. Amazing!

While my head was swirling with all of this, I turned around and saw our Canadian "30-steps and breathe" friends who Becky and I had met the day before. We were so excited to see each other there at the Sun Gate. We rejoiced and took pictures together, celebrating that we had all made it, against all odds. Despite sickness, or not being the youngest hikers out there, or not being the fittest hikers out there, or whatever else, we had made it. We laughed about the monkey stairs and how they had to put those right at the end as if we hadn't been through enough torture already. We took pictures together and celebrated our victory with our Canadian friends, and once again I offered gratitude for the help these ladies had been to us on our journey.

After a few minutes, Miguel said time was up, we couldn't wait any longer at the Sun Gate. He had a pretty strict schedule to keep to get us through the Machu Picchu tour and to our bus on time. This was fine with me because despite the joy and excitement of making it to the Sun Gate, I was still feeling completely awful and wanted to get to the bathroom as soon as possible. So we picked up our hiking poles and kept walking. The trail from the Sun Gate to Machu Picchu was slightly downhill the whole rest of the way. No more steps, no more uphill. I was starting to think I just might survive. The only problem now was that Machu Picchu was obscured by a thick layer of clouds. Did we come all this way, hiking for four days, only to go home with pictures of clouds?

We started walking down the trail from the Sun Gate and after about five or ten minutes, Miguel frantically rushed us all to one side. Apparently the clouds were shifting and the citadel was visible. We had no time to ogle the view, though, with Miguel shouting, "Get together! Get together!" He, Saul and Yossep quickly grabbed some of the group's cameras to take pictures but the clouds kept moving. By the time they took the pictures, the clouds were back in place. We laughed and continued down the trail again. This same song and dance happened two or three more times as we neared Machu Picchu. Each time Miguel would get so excited and tell us to get together quickly. Each time the clouds rolled right back in, just as we managed to get in place.

Despite our inability to get any photographic proof, we were gradually getting closer to our goal. Little by little, the clouds were dissipating until finally, in front of us in all its glory, was the Machu Picchu citadel. Just as it appeared in all those pictures, right there in front of us.

After four days of arduous hiking, the last few miles the hardest, we were here and the clouds had parted so we could see it all. The citadel was much, much bigger than I had expected. Pictures just can't capture the scope and grandeur of Machu Picchu and the surrounding lush green mountains.

That morning when I woke up sick, I wanted to give up. In fact, I believe if I'd had an easy way to get out of hiking those last few hours, I would have. Even if it meant giving up on seeing Machu Picchu. But I had no other option, so I pressed on. And eventually, the clouds cleared. Another lesson from the Inca Trail: no matter how bad or how dire the circumstances seem, the clouds will clear eventually. We just need to hold on and have faith while we wait it out. It may take an eternally long time, and the waiting process may be terribly uncomfortable, but the clouds will clear and when they do, the view will be glorious.

Chapter 19: Miracles Happen

"For the first time since dropping out of graduate school, I remembered an unpleasant weekend spent struggling to comprehend the philosopher Immanuel Kant's explanation of the difference between calling something beautiful and calling it sublime. Nowadays, we throw around the word 'sublime' to describe gooey desserts or overpriced handbags. In Kant's epistemology it meant something limitless, an aesthetically pleasing entity so huge that it made the perceiver's head hurt. Machu Picchu isn't just beautiful, it's sublime." Mark Adams, Turn Right at Machu Picchu

I really had no business hiking the Inca Trail. It was insane. I'm not strong enough. I'm not athletic enough. I'm not adventurous or go-with-the-flow-y enough. When Kellie and I were in Mexico and she asked me where we were going to celebrate my 40th birthday, I wasn't really in a frame of mind to be making major decisions. The man I loved had died just six weeks before and I wasn't really doing well, emotionally. I really shouldn't have been making choices at that point which would be so life changing. And yet, I did. When Kellie asked, I heard myself tell her we were going to Machu Picchu, and that was it. We didn't stop to realize that I was not in the right frame of mind to be making such a life-altering decision, I just made it. And then there was no way out.

When I upped the ante and decided we were not just going to Machu Picchu, but we were, in fact, HIKING for four days to get there, I don't know what my excuse was for that decision. Temporary insanity of some sort. But again, once it was said and decided, that was it. There was no way out. I read enough articles to know that not everyone who sets out to hike the Inca Trail makes it to Machu Picchu. People who are much more athletic and fit than me couldn't complete the hike, so failure was a very real possibility.

And yet, that didn't happen. I made it to the end. My feet walked every step of that trail and despite the fact that I arrived at Machu Picchu late, exhausted, sick, and utterly spent, I still made it. I got there. That is nothing short of a miracle. Saul told me many times along the way that "all things are possible on the Inca Trail" and this I know to be true because I walked it and I made it all the way to the end. I also know that miracles happen, because the fact that I survived the trail was a miracle. I made it to the top of two mountains and to the bottom of valleys and miles and miles in between. When my body wanted to stop, my mind said, "Keep going." When my body and mind wanted to stop, my heart said, "Let's go."

That is the final lesson that the Inca Trail taught me: miracles happen. They can and they do. We just need to be open to seeing them.

I am so grateful for each of these lessons the trail gave me. I am beyond grateful that I had the opportunity to hike the trail—one of relatively few humans who have had the opportunity to experience walking that path, which has existed for roughly 550 years. What a miracle that such a trail still exists, and I had the privilege of walking it. What a miracle that I was put into a group with the three best Inca warriors on the planet, who kept me alive and kept me going all the way to Machu Picchu. What a miracle that I got to the end, despite feeling so sick, and was able to tour and experience the beauty of the Machu Picchu citadel.

I set out on the Inca Trail knowing that God had placed me there, at that point in my life, for some particular reason. I didn't gain eternal spiritual enlightenment (whatever that is), but I know I was put on that trail, in part at least, to learn the lessons I have listed here. I will never know everything in life—karaoke won't teach me that, nor will hiking the Inca Trail. But I have learned some things, and for that I am grateful. The Inca Trail has taught me well, and will forever be a part of me.

Made in the
USA
Columbia, SC